Outdoor and Experiental Learning

Outdoor and Experiential Learning

An Holistic and Creative Approach to
Programme Design

ANDY MARTIN, DAN FRANC and DANIELA
ZOUNKOVÁ

GOWER

Published by
Gower Publishing Limited
Gower House
Croft Road
Aldershot
Hants GU11 3HR
England

Gower Publishing Company
Suite 420
101 Cherry Street
Burlington,
VT 05401-4405
USA

Andy Martin, Dan Franc and Daniela Zounková have asserted their right under the Copyright, Designs and Patents Act, 1988 to be identified as the authors of this work.

British Library Cataloguing in Publication Data
Martin, Andy
    Outdoor and experiential learning : an holistic and
    creative approach to programme design
    1. Outdoor education 2. Instructional systems – Design
    3. Experiential learning 4. Educational games 5. Management
    games 6. Employees – Training of
    I. Title II. Franc, Dan III. Zounkova, Daniela
    371.3'84

    ISBN 0 566 08628 X

Library of Congress Cataloging-in-Publication Data
Martin, Andy, 1962-
    Outdoor and experiential learning : an holistic and creative approach to programme design / Andy
    Martin, Dan Franc and Daniela Zounkova.
        p. cm.
    Includes bibliographical references and index.
    ISBN: 0-566-08628-X
    1. Outdoor education. 2. Experential learning. 3. Holistic education. I. Franc, Dan. II.
    Zounkova, Daniela. III. Title

    LB1047.M295 2004
    371.3'84--dc22
                                                                            2004047313

Cover photograph © Michal Stránský

Typeset by IML Typographers, Birkenhead, Merseyside
Printed in Great Britain by MPG Books Ltd, Bodmin, Cornwall

Contents

List of Figures

Acknowledgements

The authors would like to thank:

- The board and staff of *Prázdninová škola Lipnice* (Vacation School Lipnice or VSL), part of Outward Bound Czech Republic, for their co-operation in allowing us to publish the book.
- Vladimír Svatoš, the former Executive Director of *Česká cesta* (Czech Way), the Professional Development Programme (PDP) part of Outward Bound Czech Republic, for his support throughout the project and assistance in writing the Preface and the section on application of methods to PDPs.
- The many staff and volunteer instructors/trainers who have helped to evolve the methods and games; in particular Zuzana Paulusová for her knowledge of dramaturgy, David Kremer for his helpful comments about the games, and Zdeněk Beneš for the majority of the photos that illustrate the book.
- The editors of *Zlatý fond her I & II, Instruktorský slabikář* and *Sborník instruktorského kursu*, previous books published in Czech about the games, methods and programmes used to create and prepare courses.
- Associate Professor Jan Neuman, Head of the Outdoor Sports and Outdoor Education Department, Charles University, Prague, who was involved at the early stages of the development of VSL and also collaborated in writing the section on outdoor education in the Czech Republic.
- Dr Sarah Leberman, Bill Krouwel and James Neill for their collaboration in developing the theoretical aspects of the first part of this book.
- Lenka Martinová (Andy's wife) for her help with translating, Ellen Martin (Andy's mum) for proof reading, and Brigit Eames for formatting the book.

Preface

Vladimír Svatoš
FORMER EXECUTIVE DIRECTOR OF OUTWARD BOUND – ČESKÁ CESTA

ANO, JE TÁDY MOST. ALE MY JSME ZVYKLÍ HLEDAT SI SVOU ČESKOU CESTU.

Yes, there is a bridge over there. But we're used to finding our own Czech way.

Cartoon courtesy of Vladimír Rencín

'These Czechs must be strange, why don't they use the bridge?' Perhaps it's some sort of national obsession to keep looking for original, if uncomfortable, ways at any price even when much easier ways have already been created. Let's face it, we like finding new unusual ways. Yes, sometimes it means extra effort to rediscover not-so-new paths that, as it may turn out, others have already beaten some time ago. This phenomenon has deep natural roots that become obvious by having a quick look at Czech history.

Between 1948 and 1989, the Czechoslovak communist regime, sponsored by the Soviet Union, kept closed virtually all communication channels with the outside world. 'Bridges to civilisation' that could have been used to let people travel in and out or to let new information, technology or cultural influence flow in, were all torn down. The men and women behind the 'iron curtain' had to rely on home sources, often inadequate or even distorted by the socialist government. The only way to be something other than a sheep in the grey manipulated crowd was to become creative and look for one's own ways. With only very limited resources, the Czechs were discovering technology and ideas similar to those of expert teams in the West, but in quite different conditions. The resulting products of this 'do-it-yourself' approach were often comparable to products of known brands. The call of the day was, 'If you want anything other than sub-standard coming out from the communist producers, you have to develop and make something yourself.' Therefore, many Czechs ended up 'crossing the river', while the world was 'wandering on the bridges'. One positive effect resulted: it made us go off the beaten path and develop our creativity. Many original – if often slightly bizarre – ideas and products were born. Rather usual things ranging from kitchen drawers, whole family homes to complete manufacturing ideas were often made using this DIY approach. However, a few of them were world-class inventions: polarography (Jamomir Heyrovský received a Nobel Prize for this method of analytical chemistry), contact lenses and laminated cross-country skis.

Experiential education has been touched by this creative source as well. The Czech version is an innovation originally developed by a group composed of psychologists, educators and sports instructors, but also artists, physicians and students. They had not identified with the regime-supported mass 'crowd' educational approach and instead were looking for an area where healthy individual development would be possible. Empowered by the Greek ideal of *kalokagathia*, a harmonious development of body and soul, they created a unique approach to experiential education – an unusual school founded on an holistic principle.

The philosophical background, the use of the dramaturgy concept in its methodology and the scope of its practical activities can positively influence the field of experiential learning. Annually, we are reminded of this fact during the international *Intertouch* courses that take place in the Czech Republic and abroad, and during the work of our instructors in international teams for the European Institute of Business Administration (INSEAD) MBA programmes in France and Singapore. Bill Krouwel (1994, p.141), an English outdoor management development consultant, suggested that:

> The Czechs have much to teach us about how to use the outdoors and related experiential training in ways from which many who have been doing it much longer could learn ... Experiential training is not just an outdoor option. These days the outdoors is quite 'old hat' to many people, and at least a [range] of other challenges, especially 'real ones', can only help personal and team development.

Miloš Zapletal (translated from Holec, 1994b, p.145), experiential learning expert and author of many educational publications and practical activities, after having reviewed education literature from around the world, adds:

> And yet nowhere I found such a perfectly worked out educational system for young people, standing at the threshold of adulthood, as the one which Vacation School Lipnice created over the last few years.

Step aside from the beaten paths and stone bridges for a while and join the authors of this book on their expedition of the 'Czech way'. Get inspired by approaches and activities that you will encounter on it. Use them creatively and do not hesitate to modify them to your own needs – experiential learning courses need to fit the participants, culture tradition and geographic potentials that differ from country to country. Do not wait too long to start experimenting; without doubt, you will discover new possibilities offered by experiential learning.

Overview

This book is divided into three parts to reflect the integration of experiential learning theory and the dramaturgy approach, ideas for creative programming practice, and a collection of selected innovative 'games', mostly from a foundation of Czech-based facilitators. The book is packed with creative ideas and demonstrates how the dramaturgy approach can be used for more holistic experiential courses. It presents design opportunities to be more creative with young people, but also with a range of clients from corporate management education and training groups to older adults.

Until recently there has been a lack of availability of much information in English about the Czech style of experiential programming. This book presents material devoted to the theory and background to the dramaturgy approach, and aims to demystify and open up these techniques to those who wish to understand and try these ideas in their programmes. It also captures the essence of various innovative, novel and refreshing approaches to group activities, and offers depth and conceptualisation of these activities from a theoretical perspective.

The writing style throughout each of the sections reflects that of the individual authors and also the nature of the topics. Individual games can be picked out and used on their own; however, it is the method and framework of dramaturgy that provides the strength and power to this holistic and creative approach. So whilst we invite readers to read the book from front to back, it is also a book that can be dipped into for games, clarification of course practice and activities, or linking the theoretical aspects of dramaturgy to outdoor and experiential learning.

Part 1   Theory – methods and application

- Chapter 1 provides an overview of outdoor education in the Czech Republic and then introduces the creative and innovative methods of Vacation School Lipnice.
- Chapter 2 focuses on the theoretical development of an holistic approach to experiential education. It traces the development of an holistic model of the experiential education process, which is then linked to the method of dramaturgy.
- Chapter 3 highlights the five stages of the dramaturgy method of course design. Methods are illustrated by which instructors integrate a range of social, physical, creative and reflection activities into the 'dramaturgy wave', along with using all the senses and psychological, intellectual and spiritual considerations. An example of a specific course scenario is provided in detail.

Part 2   Practice – courses and activities

- Chapter 4 discusses a team approach to programming and gives practical implications for instructors.
- Chapter 5 discusses the logistics of running enhanced courses, in particular the application of the methods to professional development programmes.
- Chapter 6 gives specific details of how to use games in developing programmes.
- Chapter 7 provides discussion of game logistics.

Part 3   Games – description and logistics

- Chapter 8 provides an introduction to the games, explaining some of the core ingredients of the games, the outcomes/goals and classification of the 30 games into the different 'wave' sections.
- Chapter 9 describes and illustrates nine social activities.
- Chapter 10 describes and illustrates six physical activities.
- Chapter 11 describes and illustrates eight creative (art/role-play) activities.
- Chapter 12 describes and illustrates seven psychological (reflective/emotional) activities).
- Chapter 13 makes a brief summary and presents some conclusions.

Theory: Methods and Application

Andy Martin

1 *The Evolution of an Holistic Process*

The philosophy of experiential education is particularly necessary as a vehicle for change in the 21st century.
Itin, 1999, p.98.

Chapter overview

Adventure education has a number of characteristics, including a commitment to personal development, an adventure component, which need not necessarily be physical, some degree of uncertainty and risk taking, some challenge and reflection, a novel setting, a range of games, initiatives and activities, as well as the use of metaphors and debriefs. In order for these characteristics to be put into an experiential programme, special attention needs to be paid to programme design.

The first generation of outdoor adventure programmes emphasised personal growth through physical challenge and 'letting the mountains speak for themselves'. Further generations have added an intellectual dimension by processing the experience through facilitation and review. However, increasingly approaches have been advocated that balance physical, intellectual, emotional, and spiritual aspects of personal development.

This chapter provides the background to outdoor education in the Czech Republic and an introduction to Vacation School Lipnice, whose courses have for 25 years provided opportunity for personal development, using an holistic approach involving a range of challenges other than physical.

Outdoor education in the Czech Republic

EDUCATIONAL ROOTS: COMENIUS

The work of the Czech educator John Amos Comenius (1592–1670), who was known throughout Europe as the Teacher of Nations, is particularly significant in the foundation and development of experiential and outdoor education. Comenius believed in educating the whole person, similar to today's holistic education concepts. According to Comenius, it is necessary to educate the mind, the tongue, the heart and the hand. By this statement he meant that the most important experiences are the ones achieved by one's own senses. He recognised the importance of travelling as a means of completing youth education and also supported the use of 'games' and 'play' in achieving educational outcomes. Comenius concluded that a learning process began and ended with experience and that teaching and learning must be interconnected with experience in nature and must prepare for life itself. In his main work *The Great Didactic* (Comenius, 1632/1907) he argued for the importance of:

- the interconnection of theory and experience
- the interrelationship between school subjects
- encouraging self-directed and self-motivated study and problem solving.

FOUNDATION: *TURISTIKA* ACTIVITIES

Czech history has been influenced by its position in the centre of Europe. Because of this geographical position the Czech people have been susceptible to various influences over the centuries. General interest in national history and nature in the mid-nineteenth century contributed to the creation of the physical education movement *Sokol* (1862) as well as the *Turistický klub* (1888). *Turistika* activities include active movement (travelling by bike, skis, canoe or on foot), and outdoor and cultural activities (learning about nature, local history and sights and the life of local people). By the end of the century there was a rapid development of outdoor sports. The English influenced the foundation of rowing clubs (1860) and the development of water sports. From the end of the nineteenth century cycling developed rapidly. At the same time the founders of the *turisticka* movement and most outdoor sports realised the broad connection between sports in nature and character building.

At the beginning of the twentieth century it was the Anglo-Saxon influence, linked to the scouting movement of Baden-Powell, which spread across Western Europe and influenced Czech pioneers of outdoor activities. The ideals of English scouting and American woodcraft received great interest and the Czech founders adapted both movements to conditions in their country. Their intention was to change the school as a teaching institute into an institute of education.

Outdoor activities were developed in physical education programmes, sport corporations and in *Turistický klub* and scouting organisations. The term *výchova v přírodě* (outdoor education) was adopted by the scouting movement in the 1920s. A particular Czech historical and cultural phenomenon, inspired by American adventure literature and movies, involved many young people informally going tramping and camping at weekends ('youth stays in nature'). Tramping as a movement fulfilled the demands of young people for a life of freedom in natural surroundings. It created a specific culture that combined outdoor sports and activities such as camping with music and artistic creativity. In the 1920s the progressive liberal educational movement occurring in other parts of the world influenced Czech pedagogy. This resulted in summer camps, educational courses and experimental schools. Outdoor education development was also supported by the work of the writer and teacher Jaroslav Foglar. He devised models to encourage young people to develop a romantic relationship with nature and stressed the importance of working in small informal groups (Neuman, 2001a, 2001b). His philosophy is characterised by:

- influencing self, and relationships to other people
- the ability of self-control
- independent decision making.

COMMUNISM 1948–89

The Nazi occupation and Second World War interrupted these developments. Although social life and the activities of all pre-war organisations were quickly restored after the war, the Communist Party took over power in 1948 and the Soviet influence began to spread throughout all spheres of life. At this point a forcible unification of sport and youth organisations took place but, in spite of the totalitarian approach, the democratic development of traditions was never completely restrained.

In this period, interesting facets of hiking, sports and outdoor activities were being incorporated into the school curriculum. A tradition developed of 'schools in nature', ski trips and special summer courses involving elements of outdoor sports and *turistika* activities. A division of outdoor sports and outdoor education was started in 1953 at the first Physical Education Institute of Higher Education (the Faculty of Physical Education, Charles University Prague, from 1958). The programme was in many ways original, as it associated sport and *turistika* activities with group experiences, activities in natural environments and learning about the landscape. A feature of the programme was the integrated approach to education, because from the beginning it included sports, games, creative activities and learning about nature. However, the first programmes were more related to sports performance, where students were tested and measured (1957–63). Reviewing and evaluation was very limited. Learning activities/experiences involving preparing and leading tours and expeditions were then added (1964–68).

Development of these concepts was slowed down by the political normalisation, as opinions which did not correspond with socialist views were suppressed (1968–73). A need was identified for reviewing and supporting the independent initiative of students. The first information about Outward Bound was obtained in 1974 and it was clear that there were similarities in the two concepts. The next stage of development involved the application of games and creative activities (1974–86).

Besides many influences already mentioned, ecological movements involving education in, and for, the natural world began to gain momentum. The most famous is called 'Brontosaurus', which combines outdoor life with ecological education of children and young adults. Many ecological activities are also connected to the 'Union of Nature Conservation' and several 'Centres of Ecological Education' also try to link ecological and outdoor education.

Within the Socialist Youth Union organisation new experimental forms of outdoor education emerged, despite the tensions of the communist regime. In 1977, with considerable support of educators and volunteers, *Vacation School Lipnice* was started. To date more than 5000 participants have taken part in all types of courses. It began, together with the Faculty of Physical Education and Sport at Charles University Prague, to form the groundwork for modern and creative approaches to outdoor education. This evolution also resulted in an International Conference, called 'Outdoor Education', in October 1989. A sharp criticism of the political system took place, and a strategy concerning the future development of outdoor education in the Czech Republic was developed.

OUTDOOR EDUCATION SINCE 1989

The 'Velvet Revolution' (1989) changed the face of the whole of Czech society. Organisations have tried to reconnect their activities with Czech traditions that had flourished until 1948, and have also tried to preserve those positive elements that had appeared in the course of the following 40 years. Tramping and cycling are still very popular among young adults, and many small informal groups spend weekends at campsites, often co-operating with forest administration. Groups of adults and whole families continue to maintain 'simple life' traditions at log-cabin sites. Vacation School Lipnice and the Faculty of Physical Education and Sport at Charles University Prague have led experiential programme developments, and currently there are a number of other institutions where more formal facets of outdoor education can be found. These include schools, universities, civic youth organisations, ecological organisations, trade union recreation groups and commercial organisations (Neuman, 2001a, 2001b).[1]

Vacation School Lipnice

VSL is a non-profit organisation established in 1977 under the 'Socialist Youth Organisation' (the Communist Party arm for handling youth development). This was not a voluntary choice of an umbrella organisation, but rather a necessity dictated by the socialist regime. Its foundation was a result of long-term effort to establish a centre of educational value based in a natural environment. By 1977, within the central Socialist Youth Organisation the branch called the 'team of instructors for nature stays' had 300 members. The independent and non-conformist orientation of its members led to the dissolution of this body by the Communist Party, and the members were transferred from central Prague to country organisations. However, the members remained pro-active and the Central Socialist Youth Organisation prepared a conference about 'nature stays' and educational ideology. This resulted in VSL being established as the centre and organisation to explore education in nature, using the materials and experience from the previous courses. Dr Allan Gintel, a psychologist, established leadership, and a team of about 20 instructors was funded by the Central Socialist Youth Organisation.

During the 12 years to 1989 there were 96 courses with more than 3000 participants. The participants ranged from high-school to university students, but also older adults. There were regular biannual meetings of the instructor teams with over 200 people attending, including university professors, writers, scientists and artists. The Scout movement had been banned by the Communist Party very early after 1948. However, Václav Břicháček, the Czech Scout Organisation's Chairman, indicated that despite being operated under the Socialist Youth Organisation, VSL was educationally valuable and acceptable. He stated (1994, p.140):

---

[1] Adapted from an article by Turčová, Neuman and Martin (2003).

I am sure that at [Vacation School] Lipnice they created a small university in very difficult circumstances and in opposition to the Party power. It was a school of versatile and comprehensive education, different from the established pedagogical theory and official schools. It was the place where young people, under the guidance of young instructors, gathered to seek the truth primarily about themselves.

The paradoxically subversive nature of the organisation allowed access by dissidents to courses, the educational use of 'politically incorrect' themes and approaches, and a focus on individualism and personal growth. It should be noted that, whilst the emphasis of the courses during socialist times was on 'individualism', the move to a free-market economy and democratic society since 1989 has necessitated a refocus of courses on issues of 'co-operation' and working together in an increasingly multicultural society. The development of the courses has mirrored that of the programmes at the Faculty of Physical Education and Sport at Charles University Prague. The first stage involved a physical approach focused on sports, games and performance, for example softball tournaments. The next stage integrated aspects of *turistika*, tramping and camping activities. One of the founders, Dr Allan Gintel, was instrumental in implementing psychological games. In the 1980s and 1990s the variety of courses was notable, with those such as *Interes* introducing more strategic and structured games, and in the 1990s the course *Bottega* began to promote more creative aspects.

PHILOSOPHICAL ROOTS: *KALOKAGATHIA*

Whilst the roots of Outward Bound are based on Kurt Hahn's educational philosophies, VSL is based on the Greek philosophy of *kalokagathia*. *Kalokagathia* is made up of two Greek words: *kalos* – beautiful, and *agathos* – benign. In ancient Greece *kalokagathia* stood for an ideal nurture concept that featured harmonious development of outward merits and an inner world based on spiritual moral principles.

Vacation School, cut off from foreign experience and methods, was seeking its own way. The philosophical roots of its programme were far-reaching to the ancient world; in the background of many experiments was kalokagathia *as an idea of the beauty of body and soul.*

Translated from Holec, 1994b, p.145.

Its methodology aims for the balance implied in *kalokagathia*, and its philosophy runs counter to the idea of 'frontloading' (Priest and Gass, 1993), or of using developmental methodology in the service of pre-prepared learning objectives. Instead, it idealistically seeks to help people discover solutions to issues within themselves.

DEVELOPMENT SINCE 1989

VSL became an independent organisation in 1989 and following the visit of two instructors from Outward Bound in the UK, became an associate member of Outward Bound in 1991. Both organisations shared similar educational philosophies, and the international nature of Outward Bound provided the opportunity for further development. A year later, *Česká cesta* – 'Czech Way' (www.ceskacesta.cz) was founded, which is the part of Outward Bound Czech Republic that mainly focuses on managerial training and teambuilding courses for domestic and foreign companies. *Štúdio zážitku* – 'Studio of Experience' was registered as Outward

Bound Slovak Republic in November 1993 (in the year when Czechoslovakia was split into the Czech and Slovak Republics). In 1997, Outward Bound Czech Republic became a full member of Outward Bound International. Its mission is focused on experiential education, personal development and outdoor activities, all of which assist people in finding a deeper relationship to themselves, other people and the world using the method of experiential learning. The main goals of the educational and training courses are to develop an active attitude to life, to encourage acceptance of responsibility, to promote community involvement and to inspire personal growth.

All the problems and conflicts of the world are reflected in each of us and the world is a reflection of ourselves. Therefore we must seek the key to their solution from within. We are a civic organisation striving for global development of people's personality. By inducing powerful experiences and intensive human relations our objective is to help everyone to find within themselves unsuspected sources of energy, self-confidence and spontaneous creativity. We believe these are essential for an active and responsible attitude for life, society and the environment.

Translated from Holec, 1994b, p.146.

DIFFERENT TYPES OF COURSE

Each summer open-enrolment centre-based or expedition-based courses usually last seven to fourteen days for groups of 20 to 30 people. About 200 to 500 participants each year are involved in programmes filled with physically and mentally challenging games, creative workshops, discussions and periods of reflection. The open-enrolment courses are developed, and are able to evolve, for the specific needs of the individual and group. They are characterised by physical activities, but include a wide variety of cultural, social, creative and reflective activities aimed at enhancing the challenge to participants in ways other than just physical. Examples of courses for specific target groups include:

- teenagers and young adults
- 'GO' project for schools
- disabled and integration
- the 50+ age-group
- families/parents and children
- international participants.

Instructors are recruited (of whom there are over 100 with about 50 being active as of 2002) exclusively from the ranks of delegates perceived as having a potential for growth and eventually becoming an instructor. This means that instructors come from a range of experiences rather than from just outdoor skills backgrounds. However, it could be argued that recruitment just from its own courses is a limiting factor, running the risk of building a self-perpetuating insularity of approach. Only a very small core of full-time staff exists, so the voluntary instructors are absolutely vital to the continued provision of training.

Vacation School Lipnice (VSL) courses can be compared to a one- to two-week-long theatre play in which everybody is an actor and a spectator at the same time. This 'dramaturgy' is run according to a prepared scenario, but it changes according to events on the course itself. Its peaks and dynamism are based on interweaving a balance of effort and relaxation, physical and mental activities, individual and group events. The experience offers a range of social, physical, creative, psychological, emotional, intellectual, spiritual, and cultural challenges. Other outdoor education and professional development providers also use drama, theatre and storytelling activities; however, the use of dramaturgy as a method of course design is different from the traditional outdoor activity focus of many providers.

These courses aim to enrich the traditional range of outdoor physical activities with programmes aimed at developing other aspects of human personality, for example, creativity or social skills. The courses are based upon an environmental education approach about, for and in nature, where education in nature has many interlinking dimensions. Krouwel (1994, p.142) argued that the courses offered an holistic challenge that is more appropriate for 'the age of unreason', where things change quickly and group circumstances differ so much that a 'standard' course cannot meet the needs of all participants.

Anyone who has been condemned to run a series of identical courses will recognise the way in which energies are drained and observation blunted by repetition. Too often in the West, value is put on 'professionalism', a term which sometimes seems to be misinterpreted as meaning the ability to run repetitively a limited series of exercises with predictable outcomes. True professionalism, including the need to match exercises to group needs, deliver them safely and review them appropriately, is of course important, but it should be a partner for originality, not a substitute for it.

Programmes are characteristically intense, fast-moving, and full of unexpected experiences. The ethical principles and the approach taken by instructors and participants in terms of respect, warmth, empathy and genuineness are particularly important. This approach allows the instructors to respond and adapt the course games (many of which they have created) as a result of their previous experiences and the participants' individual and group needs (so that they are tailor-made). Assessing the needs of participants physically, mentally, emotionally, culturally and socially is an important element of adventure education courses. All courses have educational and developmental goals – whilst having recreational aspects in mind. This approach seeks specifically to enable participants:

• to understand themselves and their world
• to discover the power and meaning of relationships
• to improve citizenship
• to develop power of thought
• to go 'against the flow'.

INTERNATIONAL COURSES

This book has been developed as a result of an increasing interest internationally about the games and programmes created and prepared for these courses. In 1988, a group of volunteer instructors developed a new course for international participants, *Interproject*. This course ran each summer until 1993. The next course of this type, *Intertouch* in 1997, was described as follows:

Life is like an eighteen-speed bike. Most of us have gears we never use. Come take a ride with us and discover gears you did not even know about (and you do not even need a bike). Have a taste of INTERTOUCH.

The *Intertouch* course attracts a wide range of international participants and instructors, as well as Czech and Slovak nationals. *Intertouch* (www.intertouch.cz) has also been adapted for running at Outward Bound in Australia, Hong Kong and Singapore. Through its instructors the course has also impacted upon programmes in Britain, Germany, New Zealand, South Africa and the USA. A participant described the *Intertouch* course as:

A lifetime of experiences/lessons compressed into two weeks. It was like an experiment where I experienced tests of every capability I thought I had as a human being, and more. I used every sense, every skill, every limb and every milligram of energy in the shortest space of time possible. I used neurones I knew I had, and created connections between neurones that have never been used. The critical element is that this 'experiment' occurred in a 'cocoon' of safety/support/compassion/caring, allowing me to play full out. This cocoon allowed me to go on this emotional roller coaster of the highest highs and the lowest lows without wanting to get off. I wanted to stay on because I knew that during this journey of two weeks I was learning what would possibly take me two years or more in my 'normal' life. I know that this was more than an educational experience because when I try to explain the activities/learning to others, I often can't find the words. It was a wake-up call too because all of that was and is within me, I only need to tap into it.

2 *Theoretical Underpinnings of Dramaturgy*

> *Experiential education is a process through which a learner constructs knowledge, skill, and value from direct experiences.*
> Luckmann, 1996, p.7.

Chapter overview

This chapter provides a background to the theoretical development of an holistic process to experiential learning.

> *Learning always relates to what has gone before... Earlier experiences may encourage us to take risks or they may inhibit our range of operation or ability to respond to opportunities.*
> Boud, Cohen and Walker, 1993, p.8.

Experiential learning has been regarded as an active process involving the learner being placed in unfamiliar environments, outside their positions of comfort and into a state of dissonance. This lack of harmony requires problem solving, inquiry and reflection. This chapter presents in chronological order four models illustrating the development of understanding related to the experiential education process.

The final or 'holistic model' has been developed as a result of empirical research undertaken through VSL international courses (Martin, 2001d). This holistic approach then extends to an introduction of the method of dramaturgy. Analysis of the 'adventure wave' model, which involves a sequence of experiences and activities that are briefed and then reviewed, is then extended to the multiple waves of the dramaturgy – social, physical, creative and psychological. The role of aims, pushing comfort zones and reviewing of activities are also analysed as the methodological principles of dramaturgy are discussed.

The experiential education process

Experiential education involves an holistic process, which combines experience, perception, cognition and behaviour, and aims to encompass emotions, imagination and physical being, as well as intellect. The involvement of the whole person (physically, intellectually and emotionally, involving feelings and senses), prior experiences and reflection upon experience characterises, and is applicable to, all experiential learning (Andresen, Boud and Cohen, 1995). The structure of the experience, facilitation and assessment of the outcomes are key factors depending on the particular case. The Association for Experiential Education identified the following principles for facilitating experiential education (Luckmann, 1996, p.7):

- The educator's primary roles include setting suitable experiences, posing problems, setting boundaries, supporting learners, ensuring physical and emotional safety and facilitating the learner process.
- The educator recognises and encourages spontaneous opportunities for learning.
- Educators strive to be aware of their biases, judgements and pre-conceptions and how they influence the learner.
- The design of the learning experience includes the possibility to learn from natural consequences, mistakes and success.

However, just having an experience does not necessarily mean learning will have occurred. It is the reflection process that turns the experience into experiential education, often called the 'action-reflection cycle' (Joplin, 1981). Participants are able to reflect on and observe their experiences from many perspectives.

Learning from experience is far more indirect than we often pretend it to be. It can be promoted by systematic reflection, but we must treat the whole experience as relevant and not be too surprised when connections are made which, previously, we had been unable to see.
                    Boud and Walker, 1990, cited in Boud, Cohen and Walker, 1993, p.85.

Boud *et al.* (1993) proposed the following assumptions on which to base experiential learning:

- Experience is the foundation of and the stimulus for learning.
- Learners actively construct their own experience.
- Learning is an holistic process.
- Learning is socially and culturally constructed.
- Learning is influenced by the socio-emotional context in which it occurs.

The following models illustrate the theoretical development of the experiential education process, particularly related to Outward Bound.

1970s: THE EDUCATIONAL PROCESS MODEL

Walsh and Golins (1976) developed a model of the Outward Bound educational process (Figure 2.1), which began with the participant undertaking a series of physical activities and group problem-solving tasks.

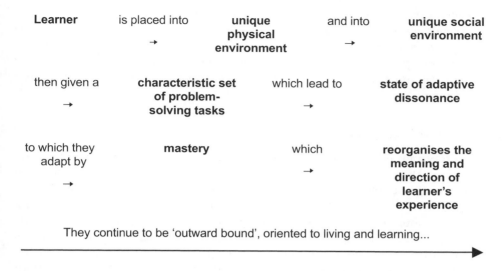

Figure 2.1   The Outward Bound educational process model

Source: Walsh and Gollins, 1976, cited in Hopkins and Putnam, 1993, p.92

This model has been particularly important in the development of an understanding of the experiential education process, as it was one of the first to list the elements of this adventure programme. Its authors suggested that the tasks needed to be introduced incrementally and have real consequence, not vicarious ramifications. The problem-solving tasks should be holistic, their solutions requiring the fullest complement of the individual's mental, emotional and physical resources. A state of 'adaptive dissonance', whereby a person has two different and conflicting thoughts, is then reflected upon. This process leads to transfer of learning to future experiences.

1980S: THE METAPHORIC MODEL

Bacon (1983) described Outward Bound as a special place, linked with transformation and change. The process is symbolic of the developmental process, a rite of passage. He believed that the impact of the environment elicits profound childlike regression in almost every participant. Bacon (1983) identified the following components of the courses: skills training, stress/hardship, problem solving, community service, reflection and evaluation, which were sequenced as a training phase, expedition phase, solo, final expedition and concluding phase. Bacon (1987) described the evolution of the educational process, with particular emphasis on how facilitation approaches had changed to ensure greater transfer of learning. He believed that initially, the focus was on the experience, 'let the mountains speak for themselves'; however in the 1960s and 1970s the second generation, 'the Outward Bound Plus model', emphasised the use of group discussion and self-reflection. He pointed out that the third generation of facilitation approaches, the 'metaphoric model', stressed the development of experiential metaphors. Traditional programmes develop powerful learning experiences surmounting mainly physical challenges in a natural setting, through which the individual builds their sense of self-worth. Kraft and Sakofs (1991, p.27) suggested that:

The philosophical underpinnings of Outward Bound education embrace the notion that learning is a complex, dynamic interplay between all aspects of the human experience. Thus it is intellectual and physical; rational and emotional; concrete and abstract; joyful and frustrating; tedious and exciting; noisy and quiet; active and sedentary… educators recognise these relationships, and through the various activities presented encourage students to embrace and appreciate learning in a multifaceted beauty.

1990s: THE ACTIVE LEARNING CYCLE MODEL

Sakofs and Armstrong (1996) described 'the Outward Bound approach to teaching and learning' as more than a set of methods and activities and that the teacher (instructor) provided an important role. They suggested the educational process has the following elements: the teacher, the experience, consequential applications of knowledge, time for solitude and reflection, adventure, physical fitness, metaphorical significance and teamwork. Also, value is placed on physical, as well as mental and emotional, experiences and on reflection upon them – through either 'solo' or group reflective time. The approach should incorporate physical and emotional safety, which allows participants freedom to learn (Figure 2.2).

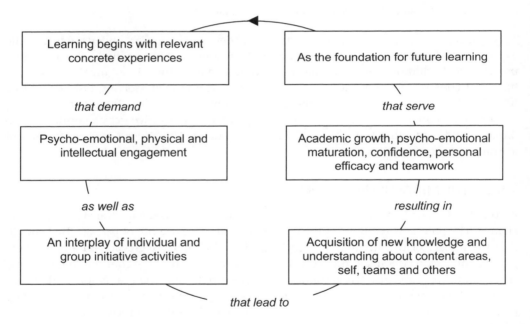

Figure 2.2   The active learning cycle

Source: Sakofs and Armstrong, 1996, p.20

2000 PLUS: AN HOLISTIC MODEL

Itin (1999) proposed a 'diamond model of the philosophy of experiential education', which suggests that experiential education involves a process linking the interaction of facilitators, participants, the learning environment and the activities. Beard's 'learning combination lock' (Beard and Wilson, 2002) also links the importance of the learning environment and a range of activities that involve all the senses with utilising peoples' learning style preferences to develop 'emotional and multiple intelligence' (Goleman, 1996).

These views support Martin's (2001d) empirical findings from participant questionnaire responses about VSL courses that the complex variables (people, processes and outcomes) involved in developing experiential education programmes are:

- Course design: An holistic approach (using dramaturgy) integrating a variety of activities (or games) involving reflection. In addition, planning what the course is about (themes, issues) and why we are doing it (instructor motivation).
- Range of activities: Balance of activities (social, physical, creative, psychological, group and individual challenge) that use all the senses and integrate reflection, emotional, intellectual and spiritual considerations. Variety provides the element of surprise and change of programme pace (rhythm). Gradual development of activities, for example, creative activity, more demanding activity, and finally independent preparation of a theatre performance.
- The atmosphere/learning environment: Physical and emotional safety; a positive and supportive atmosphere (allowing participants to play). The right setting is also important; it governs inspiration and motivation.
- The group of participants: A diverse group of participants, who are willing to participate in activities and to think about themselves and others. They need to be open, want to be there, and be able to listen.
- The instructors/trainers: The instructors' facilitation methods and experiences; quality team of individuals of different strengths, abilities and skills.

Figure 2.3 illustrates these key elements in an holistic model. What differentiates VSL courses, in comparison to traditional approaches, is the instructor's role in planning the course dramaturgy, the framing of a range of games and the development of an atmosphere that allows participants to play. The instructors, along with the development of trust and the group dynamics amongst participants, are important factors in the creation of a positive, friendly atmosphere and supportive learning environment that is physically and emotionally safe. The use of a variety of activities aims to challenge participants mentally, physically and emotionally (mind, body and soul). Outdoor activities, creative workshops and structured and non-structured games are effectively linked to produce experiential education activities that result in aspects of personal and interpersonal development.[1]

Dramaturgy as a method of course design

Dramaturgy means 'the art of theatrical production', the main task of which is to examine the links between the world and the stage. The 'dramatist' chooses themes from society and a place that reflects these themes. Pieces of work and music are then chosen to reflect these themes. Broderick and Pearce (2001) advocated indoor adventure training using drama/theatre activities. They suggested that the use of the indoors and drama is a dramaturgy approach, but fail to point out that dramaturgy is much more than just drama.

---

[1] Adapted from an article by Martin (2003).

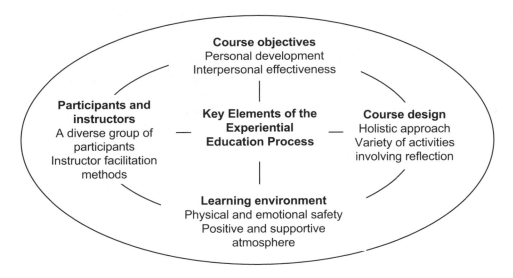

Figure 2.3   Holistic model of the key elements of the experiential education process

Source: Adapted from Martin, 2001d, p.266

The outdoors is just one option, as is drama, and the use of varied media has other benefits in that it allows instructors and participants to exercise their imagination.

Many adventure education programmes have emphasised physical adventure, viewing physical involvement as necessary to complete the learning process, but in many cases this limits the challenge for participants to perceived physical risks. The role of perceived risk is an integral part of adventure education, encompassing the belief that learning is enhanced through perceived risk, including improving one's self-concept, personal growth, leadership and the opportunity for self-actualisation. However, each individual's perception of risk is different and may be physical, social, psychological or spiritual.

> *Adventure is individual and where facilitated for other's needs to be differentiated for each participant... not everybody will enjoy the physical challenge provided by many outdoor and adventurous activities.*
>
> Boniface, 2000, p.66.

A range of non-physical, structured and non-structured group activities, incorporating aspects of art, drama, music, poetry, role-play and storytelling, have been used in the development of adventure programmes, particularly in reviewing activities. The use of games and non-physical activities is also common in professional development programmes, as these activities aim to move people out of their comfort zones in a variety of ways, whilst still applying the 'experiential learning cycle' (Kolb, 1984). Gilsdorf (1995) emphasised that the focus should be on the art of combining games into thematic sequences, then framing, leading and debriefing adventure activities to maximise personal and social learning.

Dramaturgy is a method used to plan, select and then order the individual activities and other events with the goal of maximising the final course effects (translated from Holec, 1994b, p.147):

This term, known rather from the sphere of theatre, film and TV, became one of the most often-used in recent years. Dramaturgy is a method of selection and time order of the activities with the aim to reach the maximal pedagogical effect. It integrates, within itself, the questions (and also answers) concerning the participants on the course (their age, mental and physical maturity…), time and space. The key thing for all dramaturgy considerations is to determine and realise the pedagogical, educational, recreational and other aims which the course wants to reach.

A key point is that dramaturgy allows for, even encourages, changes in programme content. A different sort of professionalism is at work, one that constantly re-examines what the goals may be and rewrites the programme (sometimes on a nightly basis) to meet participants' needs. The approach resembles self-development as opposed to training in that:

- it uses outdoors (and other experiential media) to help participants develop in areas identified by participants as important
- serendipitous learning is experienced and welcomed
- it is based on holistic ideas
- there is high programme flexibility (Mossman, 1983).

The adventure wave model (Figure 2.4) (Schoel, Prouty and Radcliffe, 1988) suggests that the pattern of experiences in effective outdoor programmes is similar to a wave. The adventure wave consists of a series of peaks and valleys with periods of turbulence, excitement, activity and calm, and it has been the prevailing approach in experiential programme design over the past 20 years.

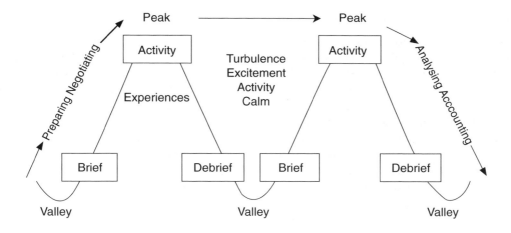

Figure 2.4   Adventure wave model

Source: Adapted from Schoel *et al.*, 1988, p. 30

While Schoel *et al.* (1988) illustrated how a sequence of activities could be briefed and debriefed as part of the 'adventure wave', Mikšíčková (cited in Martin, 2001a) suggested that dramaturgy offers not just a physical wave, but different kinds of waves (social, physical, creative, and psychological) all intertwined with associated peaks and valleys. The course design maintains a balance and a variety of challenges. It provides challenges, where people may push comfort zones socially, physically, creatively, emotionally and spiritually. Activities are generally achievable by all participants independent of fitness levels or disability. The approach allows for comprehensive self-examination, self-exploration and self-reflection of the individual in a supporting and caring environment.

A common factor is the unexpected, with the result that a kind of surrealism often features. The course surrealism takes participants 'out of this world' to an imaginary world they are co-creating. It is a 'movie-like' aspect that is developed by 'atmosphere-setting elements', which are created by the instructors and participants. These elements may be represented by the design of the centre or by minor activities staged by the instructors for the participants as spectators, but mostly by the way course activities are introduced. This introduction often involves 'framing' (Priest and Gass, 1993) games using fantasy in an imaginary scenario rather than the more real framework of traditional outdoor activity courses.

This combination of elements provokes excitement and energy; there is no difficulty in triggering streams of interesting, animated, intense discussion and debate. However, the exercises are so exciting and full that review may become an afterthought. 'It may not even be utterly necessary; over twelve days of intensive, surreal, constantly modified activity, the lessons may emerge in an unforced way' (Krouwel, 2000, p.71). The moments of subjective highest happiness and fulfilment, 'peak experiences' (Maslow, 1962), may also result in a state of 'flow', which Csikszentmihalyi (1991) suggested was achieved if an experience was engrossing and intrinsically rewarding. Peak adventure activities offer opportunities for personal growth; however, peak learning may or may not necessarily come from flow or peak experiences.

AIMS AND METHODOLOGICAL PRINCIPLES

Dramaturgy aims to produce a programme which will stimulate self-development, rather than one that will fulfil prescribed course objectives. Course objectives are deliberately wide, focusing on personal growth (individualism) and interpersonal development (co-operation). These encompass many specific sub-objectives that may emerge for individuals during the course. Research into the outcomes of these courses has indicated that personal and interpersonal development was still evident up to two years after these courses (Martin, 2001b, 2001d). Dramaturgy is seen as a vital part of the instructors' work and understanding of the experiential education process. Dramaturgy is the way to put different activities and games together to create a whole picture, a balanced result. Making the course can be an art in itself. The courses are founded on methodological principles that allow opportunities:

- for dynamic experiences
- for feedback
- to win and lose
- to experiment
- to explore social diversity
- to extend 'comfort zones'
- to explore one's abilities and skills.

EXTENDING COMFORT ZONES

The 'comfort zone' is safe, known, familiar, secure, comfortable, competent or predictable. Nadler (1995) suggested that participants in adventure programmes have choices in terms of moving out of their comfort zones by breaking through the 'edge' and of moving into new, risky or unexpected territory, or of turning back and remaining in their comfort zone. Pushing people out of their comfort zones does offer opportunities for personal growth; however, peak learning may also come from other activities and course experiences (Leberman and Martin, 2002).

At VSL the application of comfort zone theory has slightly different emphasis (Figure 2.5) (Petrová, Horáková, Mikšíčková, & Bláha, 1999):

1 The comfort zone: It is unique, an abstract shape and continually changing for every person; it has different shapes and sizes depending of life stage. Different challenges push the edge for different people.
2 The learning zone: Extending beyond the border (into the unknown and uncertainty), overcoming stress and anxiety, where one can deal with the situation and feel good about it, results in positive learning and the comfort zone being enlarged.
3 The border of comfort and learning: Stepping too far beyond the border may result in failure and the comfort zone not being enlarged (in more serious cases the comfort zone can even shrink). Transfer is the most important issue related to the comfort zone. When a person successfully pushes the edge in one activity it can help to push the edge somewhere else as well. Examples of consequences of adequate and inadequate stepping out of comfort zones include:
    – cold: getting used to it/getting cold
    – presenting in front of many people: training and boost of self-confidence/loss of self-confidence and inferiority complex
    – heavy lifting: getting stronger/injury.
4 The limit of personal abilities: We can rarely reach our real personal limits and do not usually use our whole potential. Those people who are the best in their field show the current human limits (for example, world record holder in sport or Nobel Prize-winning scientist).

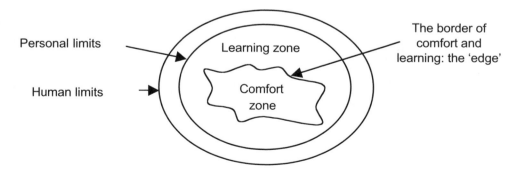

Figure 2.5   Extending comfort zones

Source: Adapted from Martin, 2001d, p. 266

REFLECTION AND REVIEW

Reflection is structured into outdoor adventure education courses in a variety of ways, for example, periods of solitude (solo), diaries or logbooks, and also reviews or debriefs. Reflection on the whole adventure experience aims to link the personal, social and environmental dimensions together. As the fields of adventure and experiential education have evolved, the use of the review for reflection about more spiritual issues has also been advocated and integrated during solo, quiet times or individual activities.

At VSL reviews are used for some activities, but may also be avoided depending on the requirements of the activity or group. Other options include providing:

- an individual reflection opportunity
- reflection in self-selected groups during 'free time'
- another activity – the debrief of which encompasses the previous activity as well
- another activity that builds on the previous activity, then in that subsequent debrief, the previous activity experience is reflected upon indirectly.

Dramaturgy requires that each activity or game is part of a whole. The wide range of powerful learning activities 'let the mountains speak for themselves' for a greater variety of participants. In this approach the taken-for-granted need for review – facilitated structured reflection – may be challenged. The reflection component, so important to experiential education, is integrated as part of the dramaturgy. This approach is in contrast to the traditional outdoor development approach, which involves a series of pre-planned activities, each followed by a review. By incorporating reflection into the whole experience, it can be argued that dramaturgy rather more accurately reflects life, as most of us reflect on our day-to-day activities but few of us actually review them.

3 *The Five Stages of Dramaturgy*

It's like rum in the cake, you can taste it in all the cake and the cake would not be as good without it.
Zuzana Paulusová, trainer of dramaturgy

Chapter overview

The uniqueness of the courses is brought about by the use of dramaturgy. This chapter reviews aims and principles of this holistic method of course design. The five stages of developing dramaturgy are presented:

1 development of the main course theme
2 development of the scenario
3 the practical dramaturgy (activity/game creation and selection)
4 the completion of the scenario
5 the dramaturgy on the course.

The dramaturgy wave illustrates not just a physical wave, but also social, creative, and reflective/emotional waves. The flow of the peaks and troughs and freeform nature of these waves are linked together under the 'dramaturgy arch'. An example of a scenario from the international course *Intertouch* is included to illustrate the planning involved in integrating the elements of the dramaturgy wave.

The five stages of developing dramaturgy

Each course is unique, with instructors adapting the pre-planned scenario and reacting to the needs of the participants. The five stages of planning the course dramaturgy (Figure 3.1) are as follows:

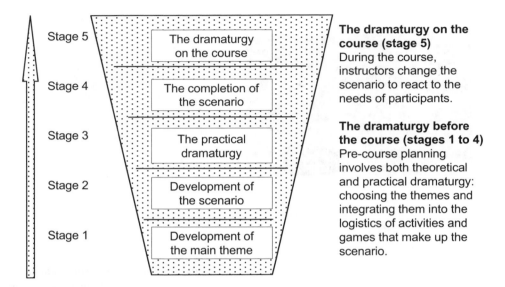

The dramaturgy on the course (stage 5)
During the course, instructors change the scenario to react to the needs of participants.

The dramaturgy before the course (stages 1 to 4)
Pre-course planning involves both theoretical and practical dramaturgy: choosing the themes and integrating them into the logistics of activities and games that make up the scenario.

Figure 3.1   Five stages of developing dramaturgy

Source: Adapted from Martin and Leberman, 2000, p.6

STAGE 1   DEVELOPMENT OF THE MAIN COURSE THEME

A main theme, which states what the course is about, represents dramaturgy at its most abstract level. One theme, or several main themes, and possibly smaller sub-themes, can present it as well. Examples might be 'Balance of opposites' with sub-themes of 'technology vs. nature; fun vs. work; spirituality vs. materialistic'; or 'Encounters' with sub-themes of 'meeting others; meeting my hidden self; meeting the world I live in'; and so on.

A well-defined course theme can serve as a point from which everything spins out – the course theme will hint about possible dramaturgy evolution, possible games and activities and atmosphere-making elements on the course. Similarly, it should be possible to link anything happening on the course back to its theme. Without a well-defined theme, there is the risk of dramaturgy without clear evolution (missing the glue of the theme) and the individual activities may lack an overall sense, however enjoyable and challenging they may be on their own.

Note that the course theme is not the same thing as course aims. Although the course theme can be formulated as an aim ('to let people find ways to reach balance in their lives in several areas'), the theme is more general and defines only a direction in which the course evolves. It provides a space for evolution of specific aims. Some of the course aims may be at a level relating to general aims of all courses of a similar type, independent of whatever theme the course may have ('to help participants identify new sources of energy, improve people skills or get fitter'). More specific aims can be, for example, 'to let people experience a transition; a closing of a period of their life and opening of another one'. The theme then needs to be developed on several levels by answering the following issues – just very generally at this point:

- What type of course is needed to fulfil the theme? An expeditionary course? A centre-based course? A winter course?
- What type of activities should be used on the course? Games? 'Real' activities? Workshops and seminars?
- In what environment should the course be run? Outdoor? Indoor? Urban?
- How will the course staff structure look? Number of experienced instructors? Only you and an assistant?
- What is the participant target group?

STAGE 2   DEVELOPMENT OF THE SCENARIO

There are two universal laws for creating a scenario:

1 It will change anyway.
2 The only certainty in life is change.

The scenario gets rewritten and changed continuously. It indicates what activities are planned for each day of the course. Creating the scenario is practically applying the dramaturgy rules and translating the themes into concrete activities. At this stage it does not involve logistics. The planning of the scenario begins with allocating time for the main activities of the course, for example the opening and closing, and activities such as solo. Parallel to this process, social, physical, creative and reflective/emotional waves, the use of all the senses, and psychological, intellectual and spiritual aspects are being developed and modified. Very often, instead of specific activities, only typology activities are placed into the scenario, for example a half-day physical game, or an activity in which the participants meet their 'shadow'. This allows for the creation of new activities to fill in the gaps if necessary. Many places in the scenario are left blank for future planning. It is important that at this stage, the course has a social peak, physical peak, creative peak and reflective/emotional peak – or at least a slot allocated for each. A wet scenario may also be considered in case of rain. The scenario with the activities is like a living organism where everything is interconnected. If you make a change it may affect the whole thing, which leads to other changes; flexibility and adaptability are very important. When planning a part of each day it is good to ask the following questions:

- What do I want to achieve? Get participants tired, calm them down, touch them emotionally, cheer them up, and so on?
- How do I want to achieve it? What sort of activity could be used to get participants to develop a particular atmosphere?

STAGE 3   THE PRACTICAL DRAMATURGY (ACTIVITY/GAME CREATION AND SELECTION)

The practical dramaturgy is the development of the different types of activities and games or the selection of existing activities to fulfil specific dramaturgy needs. The type of the activity, its position in the scenario and its impact on physical, emotional, intellectual and psychological levels has to correspond to the appropriate position of the scenario. One activity may have many different outcomes or framing depending on its place in the scenario. Therefore, developing the scenario involves a complex and holistic thinking, not forgetting the practical production planning; that is, the number of instructors, preparation time, materials, timing, people and energy levels. It is often useful to break up the scenario into 15-minute blocks, as the course days can be very intense and packed with many events that need strict time control.

STAGE 4   THE COMPLETION OF THE SCENARIO

All logistics, such as responsibilities, materials and rules for the games should be completed. At this stage there is a need to check the logistics of the rhythm and flow of the course, particularly the social, physical, creative and reflective/emotional peaks and valleys of the course. In addition, psychological, intellectual and spiritual aspects should be considered. There should also be discussion about empty spaces in the scenario for free time, reflection and review time. This is the end of the preparation phase and it is important to check to see if the themes thread together throughout all aspects of the scenario. The planning of course dramaturgy involves both process and content, and follows Kolb's (1984) 'experiential learning cycle', which is a continuous process with the emphasis on adaptation of knowledge based upon reflection of experience.

STAGE 5   THE DRAMATURGY ON THE COURSE

The fifth stage is the dramaturgy as it takes place on the course. This involves observing and reacting to the participants' needs, which requires considerable facilitation skills. The participants may come to the course with conflicting themes, which become difficult to react to, and difficult to adapt to the scenario. There are also the practical issues of weather and accidents that may prevent the scenario continuing as scheduled. In addition, reviews may need to be longer due to the impacts of major activities. The reflection and reviewing process facilitated by the instructors aims to add value to the experience and enhance personal and group development.

The dramaturgy wave

The scenario links the games and activities with the themes, waves and rhythm of the dramaturgy. The traditional adventure wave (Schoel *et al.*, 1988) sequenced a series of mainly outdoor physical activities, which were first briefed and then debriefed. However, the dramaturgy wave (Figure 3.2) offers not just a physical wave, but different kinds of waves (social, physical, creative and psychological) all intertwined with associated peaks and valleys (Martin, 2001c). Equally important is consideration of emotional, intellectual and spiritual aspects as well as utilising all the senses. The intertwining of the waves is important in maintaining a balance of intensity and rhythm during the course, for example, physically demanding games with periods of quiet and reflection (Martin, 2001c).

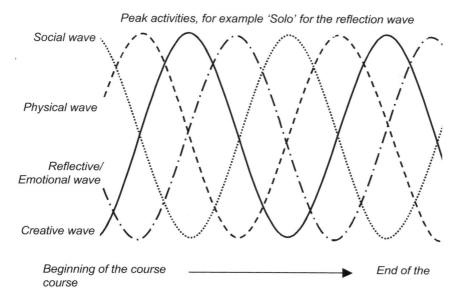

Figure 3.2   The dramaturgy wave

Source: Adapted from Martin 2001a, p.104

THE DRAMATURGY ARCH

It should be noted that the symmetry illustrated by the dramaturgy wave is an ideal. The lines in the real scenario are often more chaotic (see example scenario at the end of this chapter). If course designers aim for total symmetry, they can get badly stuck in the course design. Flexibility is the key. The activities also do not necessarily achieve the same peak, particularly those at the beginning of the course. A 'dramaturgy arch' is a connection between the activities, which comes naturally and magically. It is a planned link/flow between activities in the scenario; however it may often come naturally from the participants and that is the real magic. Figure 3.3 illustrates an example of the overall dramaturgy arch of a course and the contrast before and after the 'golden cut'. This cut is a significant period/activity in the course where the intensity/energy levels, atmosphere and/or environment changes. (This cut may be represented by a very high-energy point rather than as illustrated.) The reality of the less structured and freeform nature of the social, physical, creative and reflection waves is also illustrated under the dramaturgy arch.

DRAMATURGY EVENTS

A dramaturgy 'event' is something extra, a new idea, which is highly unusual and successful. For example on one of the last days of a particular course, the instructors announced that 'today there is no programme'. At first the participants were very unpleasantly surprised: they thought that they had been let down. After some time they realised that it did not mean that there was no programme that day, but that there was a whole day that they could fill in and

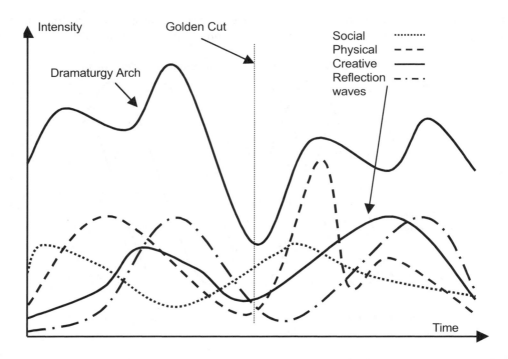

Figure 3.3   Example of the dramaturgy arch

use in very many different ways and they appreciated such opportunity for learning. Such dramaturgy events cannot be taken out of context. As the course is a 'living whole', this approach worked well in the context and structure of the particular course.

The programmes are firstly opportunities for self-development for all the people involved (participants and instructors), as well as for learning a great deal about teamwork and having fun. Put all your instructors' skills into it and the programme will work: put your whole being into it and the programme will be an unforgettable experience and learning for both you and the participants.

Significant events in the dramaturgy are often the peak activities, which may push participants' comfort zones and/or produce significant learning. These activities are briefly described below for one of the international course scenarios (*Intertouch* in Australia in 1999), to illustrate the range of games and the unique nature of each course (for more details on these activities see Part 3). A quote from a participant on the course illustrates the impact of the activity.

Social peak

Dancing Hall was a social and group activity based on music and classical dancing from successive periods: the 1930s; then the war-time 1940s melodies; 1950s rock-n-roll; the 1960s sex, drugs and flower-power music; 1970s punk-rock, and the freedom of the 1980s and 1990s. Each person had been given a role to play, which then had to be adapted, with appropriate change of dress, to fit to each decade.

'*The dance, drama, music, role plays, took me out of my comfort zone too, but I learnt most about these because I discovered I had a lot to offer to something I never knew I had the ability.*'

Physical peak

Camel Trophy was a physical activity that involved group co-operation. It was introduced by TV coverage of the real event. Normally this event involves Range Rovers travelling through difficult jungle or desert terrain, but the 'vehicles' were just four huge tractor tyres for two teams, which were to be rolled through the countryside. A number of special stages (for example, orienteering and building an 'A' frame to transport a member of the team) challenged the groups further. The final stage involved the teams building a raft to transport the tyres down a stream. The race finished at dusk with many of the participants exhausted.

'I had such an emotional time during this... it was the energy of others that helped me. I don't have to do everything on my own, accepting/asking for help is OK.'

Creative peak

Pointillism involved recreating an art 'masterpiece' using dots, lots of dots. Teams were given a painting to copy. The dots started to fill the canvases on the wall. The paint was twenty metres away, with the pictures reached by hopping, and painted by big toes, thumbs and noses. At the beginning of the game it was difficult to believe that a quality picture could be produced with just noses, thumbs and toes. However, the resulting canvas was difficult to distinguish from the original painting. Everyone had great fun and many had paint from head to foot.

'[Pointillism] helped me explore and confront hidden feelings of creativity and release them with confidence and inspiration to create more.'

Psychological peak

Labyrinth was a mentally challenging and mainly individual game, which focused on making choices of balance and harmony in participants' lives. Participants lived their lives from birth to death, with each decade of life ending after thirty minutes of real time, followed by time to reflect and write in journals. It gave everyone a chance to see his or her life through a mirror. There were opportunities to spend time working, or playing or with family, or to change the way their lives were being lived. They could be married, divorced or have children or spend time spiritually. They were also given illnesses or afflictions or spent time in hospital.

'[Labyrinth] touched real live emotions within a very life-like context.'

The scenario also involved a number of workshops, role-play activities, strategy and real games, structured and unstructured games which were framed (Priest and Gass, 1993) by instructors. They set the atmosphere, created intensity, often involving fantasy, and allowed participants the ability to play. Workshops spanned dance, drama, music and art, and the aims were spontaneity, creativity and self-discovery. The role-play activities, for example *Dancing Hall* and *Wag the Dog*, aimed to challenge participants through different roles, some similar to their own and some different. The structured games were usually physical team activities with problem-solving tasks, for example *Camel Trophy*. The non-structured games, for example *Labyrinth*, required participants to react spontaneously, be flexible and help others. Horáková (quoted in Martin, 2001a, p.106) indicated that the games allowed participants the ability to play and were important in achieving the aims of the course:

It is a game, which makes our school different from the others. A game is different than a workshop, discussion, or rock climbing, rafting or ropes course. Playing is a very common children's activity... they are spontaneous, they are really forgetting who they are if they are playing... They feel free to make mistakes and try new things, because in the game they are safe… A person can discover many new things about himself and about the others in a game. If we go deep enough into a game, we are able to leave fears and apprehensions. It brings out a lot of emotions, intensive communication and truthful behaviour as well. In a game we are solving many team or individual tasks, we are putting a lot of energy (often physical), effort and knowledge into it, we are playing different roles. It brings a lot of issues for debrief, which are connected with real life. The game is based on a story or framing, structured with rules or principles and leading into fulfilling a task or to some conclusion or peak… People are afraid to use games, because they seem to be just for children.

Although adventure education tends to emphasise physical involvement as necessary to complete the learning process, experiential education has a much wider application involving problem-solving activities and reflection. The intertwining of a range of physical challenges with activities that allow reflection, such as *Labyrinth* or a period of *Solo*, presents a more holistic approach to learning than has been advocated for experiential education.

Example course – Intertouch 2002

In this example, you will be able to see the main elements of the interaction among the course theme, the resulting dramaturgy and the final scenario. We will present the actual scenario as it really happened, not as it was planned because, as in any other course, the planned scenario was changed to some extent during the running of the course. The course was designed and run by an international team composed of Jan Lazar (chief instructor), Daniela Zounková, Dan Franc, David Kremer (Germany), Karel Černošek, Markéta Marijczuková, Sharon Hainsfurther (USA) and Abdul Kahlid (Singapore).

DRAMATURGY

The main course theme was chosen to be 'close encounters' – that is encounters of opposites, genders, generations, nations, cultures, religions, nature, outside, people, future, past, present. The close encounters were divided into four main areas, which set up the basis for the main course dramaturgy:

1 You and Me: First contact – names and faces; similarities and differences; accepting people the way they are; inspiration, learning and teaching; meeting on a deeper emotional level.
2 We and Me: How strong are we together? How can we co-operate? Roles, norms, structures; balance and imbalance in this team, group energy. What do I bring? How can I tune up to the energy of the group and use it?
3 Me and Myself: Who am I? What are my boundaries? Where am I going? From where do I get my life energy? What limits me? Where can I grow? What is the potential I didn't know about me? The 'animal in me', embracing myself – acceptance.
4 The World and Me: My place in the world. How do I use my powers in the world? What is my responsibility for the world? Embrace the world.

Each day, we identified where we were in the overall course dramaturgy, what were the themes being brought to the course and what were the key activities for the themes.

Although the main dramaturgy waves can be tracked from the scenario quite easily, the team did not work with them explicitly during the course planning. We did not draw how we would like the curves to look and then fulfil them by looking for activities, but did this process intuitively. We knew what the key activities were for particular days, which gave us a picture of the 'height' of related dramaturgy waves for that day. For example, we knew that the psychological wave would be at a peak on Day 4 because of the *Labyrinth* game and therefore it should go lower on subsequent days, to reach another peak on Day 9. We intuitively knew where the particular dramaturgy wave would develop and where the other waves should be. Using the previous example, the physical wave on Day 4 should be quite high to compensate for the psychological intensity of the day; all other waves should be very low so the participants do not get over-stimulated. This intuitive design follows the basic recommendations mentioned in the dramaturgy chapter of this book. Because of the experience of the team members, it did not have to be done explicitly.

SCENARIO

Day	Phase	Goal of the activities, themes	Key activities
1	You & Me	Participants are our guests, first encounters with the others	The interactive
2	We & Me	Preview of the course, first encounter with the group, self-presentation;	opening show Web Pages, Games without Borders
3		How does the group function? Where is the source of our creativity?	Eye for Eye, Amalda, Gateway
4	We & Me, also Me & Myself	How can I live my life? What is the role of the others in it? How does my life relate to the others?	Labyrinth of the World
5	Me & Myself	How do I function in unknown social environment? How do I function in a small intense group? How well can I use others and my resources?	Czech Dream Book
6		Same	Ditto
7		What is deep in me that I have not shared?	Dead Poets Society
8	Me & Myself	What is in me that I do not know about or use too much?	KI, Running, Guest
9		What are my limits, how many of them are real? How do I react to a major hardship?	Nexus VI, Sweat-lodge
10	Me & the World	How do I fit into the world? How do I bring my resources and my group resources to the world?	Workshops, Theatre prep
11		Same	Theatre
12		Same	Course closure

Figure 3.4 illustrates the complete scenario. Different shadings identify the main focus of each activity. Many of the games focus on more than one area; however, for the purposes of illustration one main shade is generally used.

The following is a brief description of some of the activities illustrated in Figure 3.4 (other activities are described in Part 3):

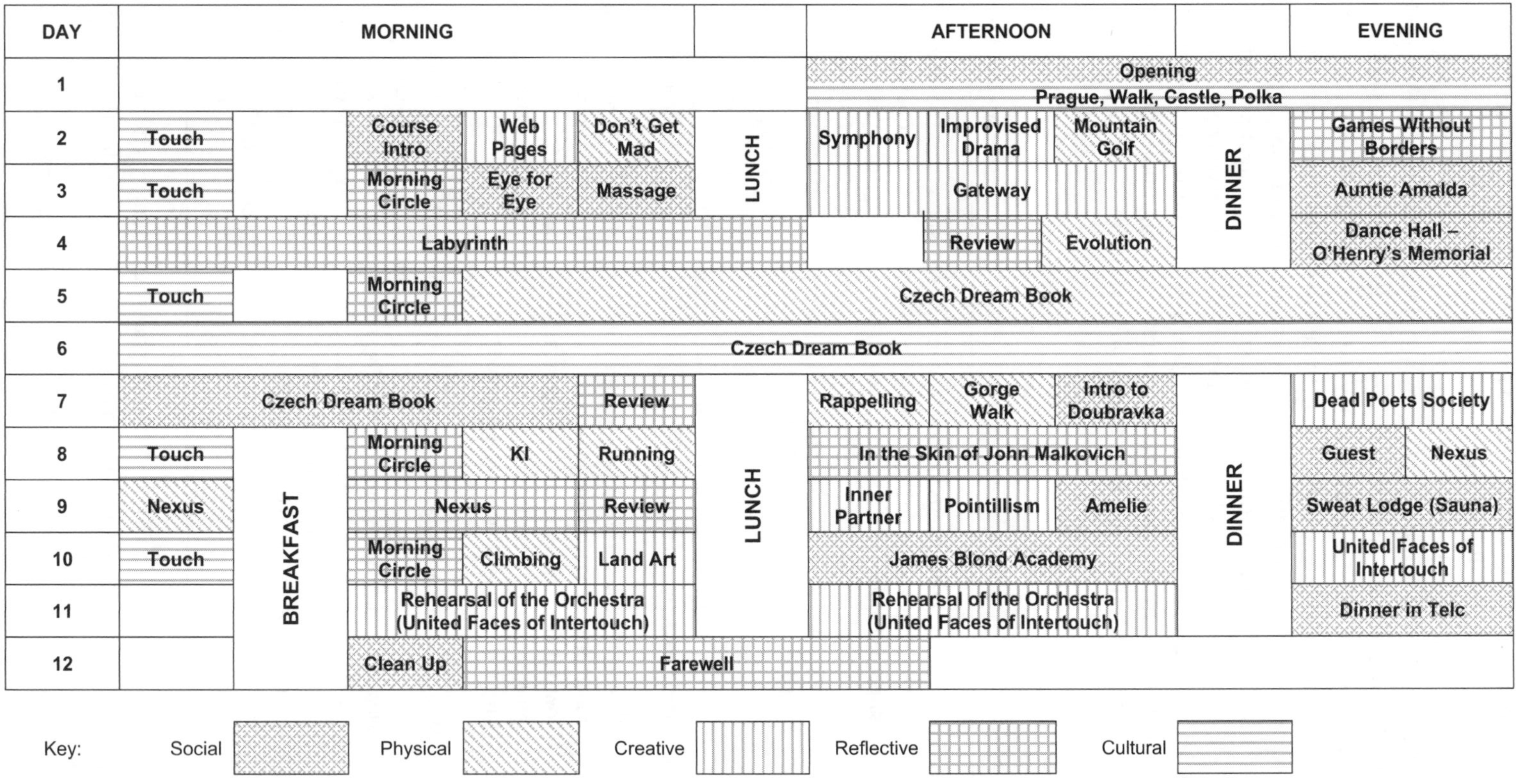

Figure 3.4 Intertouch Scenario 2002

DAY	MORNING	AFTERNOON	EVENING
1		Opening; Prague, Walk, Castle, Polka	Games Without Borders
2	Touch; Course Intro; Web Pages; Don't Get Mad — LUNCH	Symphony; Improvised Drama; Mountain Golf — DINNER	Auntie Amalda
3	Touch; Morning Circle; Eye for Eye; Massage	Gateway; Evolution	Dance Hall – O'Henry's Memorial
4	Labyrinth	Review	
5	Touch; Morning Circle		
6	Czech Dream Book	Czech Dream Book	
7	Touch; Czech Dream Book; Review — LUNCH	Rappelling; Gorge Walk; Intro to Doubravka — DINNER	Dead Poets Society
8	Touch; Morning Circle; KI; Running	In the Skin of John Malkovich	Guest; Nexus
9	Nexus; Nexus; Review	Inner Partner; Pointillism; Amelie	Sweat Lodge (Sauna)
10	Touch; Morning Circle; Climbing; Land Art	James Blond Academy	United Faces of Intertouch
11	Rehearsal of the Orchestra (United Faces of Intertouch)	Rehearsal of the Orchestra (United Faces of Intertouch)	Dinner in Telc
12	Clean Up; Farewell		

(BREAKFAST precedes the morning sessions for Days 7–11.)

Key: Social | Physical | Creative | Reflective | Cultural

- *Morning Touch* – activity in which small groups of participants prepared a wake-up activity that reflected the theme of touch in any interactive way.
- *Morning Circle* – a group meeting, during which people had the chance to have some final comments/reflections on the previous day's activities. It also allowed for various technical comments on the group dynamics, and so on.
- Quiet time – 30 minutes off just by themselves, without social interaction with others; time for reflection and relaxation.
- *Don't Get Mad* – a fun team-based running game.
- *Symphony* – a creative activity, in which participants improvised music using natural and artificial objects.
- *Eye for Eye* – a team-based strategy game.
- *Gateway* – a creative project, during which the participants created a huge gateway to the course centre.
- *Evolution* – an icebreaker just to get people moving.
- *O'Henry's Memorial* – a modification of the *Dance Hall* activity.
- *KI* – an introduction to an Aikido workshop.
- *Running* – a workshop on how to enjoy running offered by Pavla Francová, blind runner and world champion.
- *Guest* – an evening with Pavla Francová, focusing on her athletics, paintings and just life in 'another world'.
- *Inner Partner* – two self-discovery workshops based on performing arts offered by two theatre professionals.
- *Sweat-lodge* (Sauna) – after dinner, the participants created their own outdoor sweat-lodge.
- *James Blond Academy* – a team strategy game.
- *United Faces of Intertouch* – surprise theatre performance by the participants to visitors to a nearby theatre and music festival (the slot for *Intertouch* was booked many months before the course).
- *Farewell* – a set of smaller closing reflection activities.

Key principles or issues reflected in each day

- Day 1: Very typical first day – an intense and demanding opening programme that cost the team a lot of energy but managed to focus the participants towards the course and away from their daily problems and routines.
- Day 2: Our main aim was to provide a preview of what was to come. As Figure 3.4 shows, there were physical games, creative activities, a self-disclosure game, a psychological game and a fun game. Also, the game forms were different – including both structured and less-structured games, short and long activities. Running *Games without Borders*, which is an emotionally very intense activity, so early in the programme was a risk, but it worked very well. The name we gave to this day was appropriate, 'United Colours of Vacation School', as the day felt like an MTV show full of various clips, colours, experiences and emotions. Usually, the second day needs quite a bit of energy on the instructors' part – the participants' energy is only just building up.
- Day 3: It was just about time to introduce a larger and more demanding activity, which was the *Eye for Eye* team game. Thanks to the intensity of the activity, the following massages were gratefully accepted. The *Gateway* was another large project; this time it was less structured and aimed at developing creativity. The evening ended in a very open-ended activity heavily based on role-playing. (Note that on Day 2 we were running one smaller

creative activity before the *Gateway* and one smaller acting activity before *Auntie Amalda*.)

- Day 4: We were far enough into the course to bring in the first psychologically demanding game – *Labyrinth*. It was also one of the most logistically demanding activities, requiring every team member and even additional external staff. *Labyrinth* – as expected – brought out big emotions and therefore the rest of the day comprised non-demanding physical, mental and emotional activities that helped ground the experience from the morning. Also, we wanted to have a big dancing activity in the scenario and the evening of Day 4 was ideal.

- Day 5–Day 6: Just as some of the participants started to feel that things were predictable, they were told that they were leaving the current centre and were going to spend three days wandering in small groups on their own – *Czech Dream Book* – and having to accomplish several tasks. The team packed and left for the new centre, caught up on sleep, had a mid-course review, resolved some internal storming and got ready for the second half of the course. Note that this point in the course is the 'golden cut' concept in action.

- Day 7: Almost all participants returned on time and shared fantastic stories that indicated they had gathered lots of energy during the wandering days and were ready for the second half of the programme. The rappelling (abseiling) from a great rock was not originally included in the scenario, but we liked it because it made a high-level cut between the old times and the new times at the next centre in a metaphorical and experiential way. After dinner, we originally planned for *Sauna*, but it started to rain heavily so we quickly changed and presented *Dead Poets Society*, an activity originally intended for Day 9. Note that the focus and outcome of *Dead Poets Society* would be different on Day 9, as was *Sauna* on Day 7 different from Day 9.

- Day 8: The *KI* and *Running* workshops were welcome physical activities and also gave participants their first chance to meet Pavla Francová – as a guest and as an instructor. It was also another chance to have a workshop form in the programme. *In the Skin of John Malkovich* was a less-structured psychological game that left some of the participants confused. The group realised that the time of complex and demanding activities was coming. The game also showed participants that they knew each other less than they thought. The evening meeting with Pavla Francová was inspirational for many – it prepared them mentally for tackling and overcoming something that looks very hard. From the course design perspective, the evening was arranged in a different format as a lecture/workshop run by an external person.

- Day 8: *Nexus* came during the night and presented many new challenges for the participants. For the first time, they were treated negatively (of course, only as a part of the game), the game was run at night, the motivation was extremely intense and the physical aspect of it was demanding for many. These types of games can be run only after you have built up a very high level of trust and rapport with the group, so the participants know that no matter how big troubles they are in, it is all for a good reason. This activity was logistically demanding and took the resources of the entire team and several external guests as well. Also, because the end of the course was not far away, this was the last of the emotionally intense activities introduced on the course for psychological safety reasons.

- Day 9: *Nexus* ended in the early hours of the morning and everyone was given several hours to sleep. *Pointillism* came as a very welcome relief after *Nexus* – it was fun, creative, colourful and active. The *Sauna* preparation at night was one of the most energetic sauna-building activities seen on our courses; the participants were floating on the course wave.

- Day 10: The game originally prepared for the morning did not fit the group dynamics and energy. We made a fast decision in the morning, first checking whether we could fulfil the aim for the day, and four of us offered workshops with virtually no preparation – instructor creativity and flexibility in action! The afternoon's strategic *James Blond Academy* game was introduced a little too late, meaning that the participants were not accepting structured competitions any more, especially with the few little glitches in the rules we brought into the game. On the other hand, they turned the whole game into fun and enjoyed it on an unplanned and quite unexpected level.

- Day 10–Day 11: Participants were thinking that they had seen it all and nothing would surprise them. However, seeing the name of their course on official theatre festival posters – announcing that they were performing some 20 hours after getting the poster – shocked many. Because they had experienced a number of creative and performing activities, we believed that they were ready for the challenge. The group got a night and part of a day to design a theatrical piece and take care of marketing (they even managed to have a message broadcast on the regional radio station). The instructors stepped back completely at this stage and served only in support roles. The whole theatre event was a huge success, attracting a couple hundred of spectators and generating a lot of energy among the participants. In the evening no activity was presented, as the time was left open for participants to say their good-byes and prepare for their return.

- Day 12: After centre clean-up, a set of closing activities was presented, finishing by bringing back the central character of the opening, who encouraged them on their journey – just as he had at the opening. The end of the programme was emotional, yet it seemed that the participants were in peace with the end and able to see it as a new beginning for themselves.

2 *Practice: Courses and Games*

Dan Franc

4 A Team Approach to Programming

I know that this was more than an educational experience because when I try to explain the activities/learning to others, I often can't find the words. It was a wake-up call too because all of that was and is within me, I only need to tap into it.
(International course participant)

Chapter overview

The teamwork character of the course preparation brings some special needs and processes. Teams composed of six to eight instructors are put together more than six months before the courses start. Although this chapter is based on teams formed by volunteer instructors (who may have jobs other than as instructors), you can use the team approach to running programmes in other settings and organisations as well.

This chapter focuses on:

- preparation and design of courses in a team
- basic considerations when running a course in a team
- ways to adapt courses and games for the purposes of your organisation.

Preparing and planning courses

During the preparation, the team works on the basis of mainly weekend meetings, which happen every four to six weeks. Therefore, each team would have around four to six meetings before the course starts. These meetings are where most of the common planning and work on the scenario happens, but instructors work a lot individually or in smaller teams in between the meetings. Most of these team meetings are planned well ahead of time so people can fit them into their naturally busy schedules. The preparation process is a great learning opportunity for everyone, as well as social time spent with friends and inspirational people. Self-growth, self-development, deep encounters with other people, creation of new activities and approaches and just fun are some of the main reasons why many people work as volunteers on the courses.

TEAM INDEPENDENCE

One of the reasons for the creativity of the approaches described in this book is the relative external team independence. While every organisation has different policies and possibilities, it may be worth considering the scope for the creative independence of your teams. Before starting the design, every course needs to be approved by the management team. Once given the green light, it is the chief instructor who has the main responsibility for running a successful and safe course. Whatever new games, methods and approaches the instructors want to run, they can, as long as the chief instructor permits them. Therefore, it is a key decision for the management to approve a chief instructor, as she/he is the most significant means of ensuring the continuity and integrity of its courses. The chief instructor must be able to understand the organisation's philosophy and methods, and bring them to life on the course.

However, let us also think of internal team independence. The design of these courses is very creative, so their preparation needs to be somewhat organic, not constrained by many rules, filled with loads of fun for the team and involving an occasional pushing of limits. In this book, we provide you with a lot of theoretical background and practical models to use in your own course design and running. However, these are just an inspiration. Keep in mind that for design of truly 'creative' courses, rules constantly need to be bent, new paradigms need to be created and sometimes doing things just intuitively works in teams that are well tuned.

There are examples of courses that did things right. The result was a professional course, yet the participants perceived that something was missing. That something comes out of the internal team independence and its freedom – freedom to have fun, to create totally new things, to defy some rules within the basic boundaries. The course model we present in this book is very much about games – make sure you do not forget how to play yourself.

INSTRUCTOR ROLES

An ideal team should consist of a variety of characters, so they each bring something unique and different to the team. You need people who are good at organising physical activities as well as people who are soft-skill-focused (creativity, drama, psychology, environmental issues and philosophy). You should also look at team roles. According to a classification presented by Belbin (1981) these are innovator, investigator, chair, shaper, monitor, evaluator, team worker, organiser and finisher. You need to recognise individual learning styles; for example, are people 'larks' or 'owls'? Some people love to get up early and do morning yoga and then they are tired by early evening; others are useless in the morning, but happy to run the evening meetings and activities. You can also look at the compatibility of the team on a personality level – some teams administer their own Myers-Briggs Type Inventory (MBTI) questionnaire to their instructors to find the strengths and weaknesses of the team as a whole on a personality level. The team diversity is ideally achieved by combining the following parameters:

- Demographics: gender, age, occupation (if not full-time instructor), marital status
- Personal energy: extroverts, introverts, 'show-people', 'serious people'
- Team role preference: leaders, followers, process controllers
- Creative process role preference: idea generators, idea carriers, critics, 'down to earth' people, 'in the clouds' people
- …and many more parameters, depending on participants and course type.

The following list reflects the traditional course roles. Although every organisation's formal role division is different, it can help in setting up your team with regard to responsibility division.

- Chief instructor: Responsible to the organisation management. They create the original course idea, defend it during course approval interviews, compose the team, design the course preparation schedule and are the ultimate decision maker.
- Deputy chief instructor: They take on every task of the chief's work in case the latter is not able to fulfil their role for any reason.
- Qualified instructors: The instructors with formal training certification represent the core of the team. They run main activities and provide guidance to trainees.
- Trainees: One to three team members who are still working on their formal instructor qualifications. Depending on their experience, they run fewer activities (if at all), serve more assistant roles and tend not to run key activities.

EXTERNAL TEAM MEMBERS

Inviting other people to help run the course at some stage often enhances the course rhythm in the eyes of participants. The guests will not disturb the group dynamics and intimacy of the participant and instructor group if they are introduced to the course in a sensitive manner and with a clear definition of their role. The most common examples are:

- External specialists: They perform tasks that team members are not qualified to do; for example, complex physical outdoor activities or psychologically-oriented activities.
- Course partner: A senior instructor who observes and may help with activities for a couple of days on the course. The partner's role is to provide feedback to the team on how they are doing and to provide a summary of the course and team to the organisation office. This function is especially useful if the team enjoys some independence from the organisation. The partners are usually a positive addition to the team and, unless you have another feedback mechanism, we recommend using them. Their focus is not criticism, but a third

person view, which is often very hard to achieve by the instructors who are totally submerged in their work.

TASK ROLES

These roles can be served by anyone on the team, but should be clearly defined during the course preparation. Although any of these responsibilities can be delegated to other team members, the task role division is important in order to have one person responsible for a particular area. Any number of these roles can be combined. In some settings staff members external to the core team may perform these roles.

- Logistics: Movement of major materials; making sure the course programme is achievable with available resources, such as food supplies.
- Material care: Completing the material list during the design and preparation stage; collecting and transporting the material; material check during and at the end of the course.
- Medic: Medical contact for participants; reporting issues from participant medical declarations to the team and suggesting treatment of participants needing special care (both physical and psychological); care of the medical material on the course; keeping the medical journal on the course.
- Participant communicator: Sending out letters and other communications to participants during the preparation (if the team performs this function).
- Centre communicator: Single-contact point for communication between the course staff and the staff managing the centre in which the course takes place.
- Recorder: If the course is being recorded (photos, video or a detailed journal – that can be published day by day as a special course newsletter), this person is responsible for creating and presenting the record.
- Promotion manager: If the course runs its own promotion, besides the core promotion done by the organisation, this person is the ultimate manager of it.

Depending on the course set-up you may also want to create other roles; for example, a 'Duty Person' or 'CD' (Co-ordinator of the Day), who is not the chief but rather someone who co-ordinates, and passes information to both team and participants. They also exchange information among instructors running activities, know where people are, make sure everything is ready, and that the day is running smoothly and on time! They co-operate with the 'CD player' – a participant taking on a similar role among the participants. They make the information flow from and to both sides. The CD also allocates tasks and responsibilities and gives space to other instructors so they can be creative. At the same time keep in mind that it is not an individual process, but a team effort.

INSTRUCTOR SPECIALISATION

An ideal team is composed of instructors who are skilled in complementary areas – not necessarily with one specialisation per person. If a specialisation required by the programme is not present in the team, a guest instructor can be asked to come on the course to help with the particular activity.

- Activity-related specialisations: arts, performing arts and drama, reflective/emotional activities; physical outdoor activities,
- Participant-related specialisations: instructor skilled in a physical/psychological discipline or in group dynamics.

PRE-COURSE PLANNING

The pre-course planning involves a lot of design work, even if you are repeating an existing course. Most courses should be redesigned to some extent if you want to repeat them, because you want to make sure the course fits your specific participant group, specific instructor team, the time of year and the location with its facilities and programme elements. Either the chief instructor, a part of the team or the entire team can undertake this design process. Once the team is formed, it is useful to bring it together socially to do some teambuilding. As your team will be designing the course it should be tuned together to some extent. Ideally, your pre-course meetings would be full of creative ideas and interactions among friends – producing a lot of work along the way as well. Try to think of ways to make your pre-course meetings enjoyable and fun, thus opening up the gates for team creativity. It may mean preparing special surprises and/or games for the rest of the team, agreeing on non-working teambuilding meetings, or having the meeting in unusual places, and so on.

While every course has its main theme, additional course themes are developed amongst the team of instructors. Initially they bring their own ideas for additional themes. It is also worth discussing how the main theme relates to personal themes of individual team members, and possibly adding sub-themes based on their input. The team then looks for links between these themes and uses this input in influencing the development of the main course theme. The dramaturgy evolution then involves the team planning to fulfil the course theme(s). At this stage, you will need to decide what form to use to meet the course themes. For example, meeting the aims of a physical wave somewhere on its peak may take a form of trapeze jump for teenagers and a bike trip for seniors. The team can split into small groups that work independently to prepare or design key activities that already have a space in the scenario. As Paulusová states (translated from Knotek, 2001, p.14): 'if you can't find a form for a theme, your best choice is not to force the theme into an inappropriate form, because a bad form will ruin even the best theme'. The process of completing the scenario may go in rounds – when you think the scenario is completed, you may find an inconsistency and end up redoing part of it. Fine-tuning the scenario is one of the key parts of the course design, because the scenario in its completed form drives the pre-course preparation and is what brings the course dramaturgy to life.

While you are completing the scenario, you also have to check it from a logistical standpoint to make sure you have resources to run the planned activities. If you run the course with a team of instructors, you have to assign an 'activity chief instructor' to every activity, that is a person responsible for running the activity (see Chapter 7 for more on the staff roles whilst running activities). Also, it may be necessary to decide who will participate on each activity and in what role, and who will participate in the game preparation. This decision is extremely important, as it will show you how many instructors are free during the activity to prepare something else. Check the scenario to make sure that participants and the team get enough time for sleeping and eating and also time off. Further logistical checks should be made to make sure you have the material you need for every activity at the time it should be running and that it is not taken from preparation of a subsequent activity. Check that participants are able to participate in the activities from a technical perspective. If they are too tired from the previous activity, or do not have any dry shoes left, then a particular activity will not work for them. When the scenario is completed, full-scale course preparation can begin, that is gathering all materials, scouting the terrain and creating various activity props.

On the first look, the process of creating the scenario looks awfully complex – combining course goals, the dramaturgy/wave requirements, the resources available, the staff and the logistical conditions. However, experienced teams often do this process intuitively. They do not draw the dramaturgy lines on flipcharts, examine all possible threads or check every activity against every other activity to see if there is a desired contrast in the dramaturgy. If you and the team members have the basic model in mind, you can go through the scenario creation process painlessly, with fun and even bringing in new ideas... you will note that your intuition probably follows the dramaturgy model. During the intuitive design you just need to have a mental check against the models from time to time to see if you are still on the right track. Often it is sufficient if only the course chief plus perhaps one instructor are skilled in the models – they can use the very creative (that is, unlimited by conditions) resources of the less experienced staff members and just steer the discussion in a productive direction. The more experienced you become, the less these checks are needed – and the more you can focus on the creative design work rather than on following ideas from guidebooks.

Running the course

We will not go into every detail describing the teamwork on the course, as it greatly depends on local practices, team set up and many other factors. However, two areas need mentioning:

1 updating the scenario
2 team meetings – the cornerstone of teamwork on the course.

UPDATING THE SCENARIO

The scenario, in the version which exists before the course, seldom survives the entire course in its original form. The team can never fully estimate the real needs of the participant group and the actual group dynamics on the course and is always forced to update the scenario to reflect participant needs. The team constantly needs to observe the following areas and be ready to incorporate any changes into the scenario design:

• Theme evolution and group dynamics: There may be 'group themes' or issues that need addressing by choosing something different from the originally planned activity. If there is tension in the group and an unspoken conflict is boiling under the surface, introducing a game with an element of conflict may bring this topic up, but at an intensity that you are not able to manage. In such a case, a better decision may be to uncover the group dynamics using other means before such a game.
• The participant energy level: Sometimes an activity may be too hard or too easy energy-wise for the participants.

- Team readiness: If you run the course in a team, you have to be prepared for unexpected developments – your team will have its own dynamics that will be affecting the course. Do not hesitate to adjust the programme if the team is not ready for whatever reason to run an activity.
- Logistical readiness: Similarly you may find out that the material you wanted for the activity is not available, or that the environment in which you wanted to run the game is not accessible any more.
- External social events: For example, you might find out that the access to the field you planned for a big running game is suddenly not available and have to decide on another activity. However, the external environment can influence your courses on a global scale – for example, the tragic events of 9/11/2001 caused two professional development courses to change their scenarios immediately.
- External natural events and weather: It does not necessarily have to be a flood, but an unexpectedly closed road may result in major shifts in the scenario. Weather is also a big shaper of possible changes in your scenario.

Some decisions on combining the activities are obvious. We won't stay indoors in the centre for the whole day (even if we prepared indoor activities), when the weather permits great outdoor activities; but instead will run a combination of indoor and outdoor activities.
(Jirásek, translated from Prázdninová Škola Lipnice, 1990, p.14).

The following are the main risks in scenario planning that you may encounter, which would also give reason to change the scenario.

- Inappropriate place of the game in dramaturgy: One of the most common mistakes on courses is that you follow a certain dramaturgy wave for too long, ignoring the other waves. Running three creative games in a row probably is not the best idea – unless you need so much creative energy in the course and your dramaturgy is set up in a way that it is able to keep participants' attention high during all three. Similarly, a situation may occur when you neglect a particular dramaturgy wave for too long. When you need to change the scenario during the course, the dramaturgy configuration often changes as well. However, you have to make sure that in the overall big picture, none of the dramaturgy waves you planned for are eliminated, unless you are absolutely sure they do not have a place on the course.

The two following issues occurring while you are running games may result in changes in scenario as well:

- Unplanned activity outcome: During the course, you may realise that you are following a certain theme with your game, but during the game it is obvious that participants are not interested in this theme and instead put their own themes into the activity. For example, you planned *Triffids* to be about personal challenge, but your participants actually do not accept the challenge and watch through the blindfolds. You also notice they enjoy just being together in the forest at night, holding each others' hands and seeing their entire team. It is obvious they needed a team experience, rather than an individual challenge. This situation actually happens in a very mild form during every game and is generally positive, as you want to work with the existing group dynamics and needs, rather than forcing its development. However, in extreme cases, the entire game may have a totally different outcome from what you expected. Your best bet is to live with it and not try to force the participants to come back to the original aim of your game either during the game or afterwards.

- Energy mismatch: Sometimes the participants have not enough or too much physical or mental energy for the game. The problem starts if you realise this only after you started the game. Recommendations for handling this situation would be the same as in the case of adjusting the game flow, as described above. However, if the game requires more energy than the participants have, they sometimes push themselves – perhaps even unconsciously – to complete it. Sometimes the best learning moments and peak experiences come out of this for them. Similarly, if the energy of the participants is much higher than they need for a particular game, the next game (rather than adjusting the current game) may fix it.

TEAM MEETINGS

Usually, every day is planned after the last programme of the preceding day, which requires nightly team meetings from the team.

- The day is reviewed activity by activity, presenting the main highlights regarding the participants, the activity logistics and the instructor team co-operation. Then conclusions are drawn regarding the group dynamics. Also, if there are participants with special needs, they are discussed.
- The second part is checking the next day's scenario to see if it fits the current situation. If a change is necessary, the team discusses how to make the change.
- If you realise you cannot use an activity planned for the next day, do not try to create something from scratch – it is too late. You will need to choose another already existing activity. The easiest way – besides selecting a well-known activity – is to take another already planned activity from later on in the course that may serve the purpose better than the originally planned one. Make sure though that the activity chief is able to prepare the game in time. Also, you will face the problem again when you need to fill the hole in the scenario that was created by moving the activity forward in the course. Some teams bring a reserve bank of common well-known activities that are universal enough so they can serve multiple purposes (such as *Ecosystems*), even though the original scenario did not plan for them.
- Once the scenario for the next day is complete, the logistical briefing begins. Every activity chief provides an overview of the activity logistics and schedule, and confirms with the activity staff their availability. Meeting times are then set up with them for full briefing (ideally they should have already been briefed). The goal at this stage is to make sure that every team member knows their individual duties for the day, the exact schedule of activities and their chiefs.
- Finally, the chief instructor closes the preparation, which may mean time for other feedback. Ideally these meetings should happen daily, and because they take place at night, require skilful management to ensure they are as concise as possible.

5 *Running Enhanced Courses*

*It was like an experiment where I
experienced tests of every capability I
thought I had as a human being, and
more. I used every sense, every skill, every
limb, every milligram of energy in the
shortest space of time possible.*
International course participant

Chapter overview

This chapter provides details of how courses can be adapted to specific environments using a
team-based facilitation approach. It discusses how games can be integrated with existing
programme elements for both centre-based and expedition-based courses.

The application of the VSL methods to Professional Development Programmes (PDP) is
also discussed, and two example scenarios are provided to illustrate how these courses can be
enhanced.

Running enhanced courses in your organisation

You can run courses enhanced by games and dramaturgy anywhere – even though it may look like the system is difficult to transfer to environments other than the one in which it was created. The following strategies have been used to address concerns when running games internationally (in Australia, Britain, Hong Kong, New Zealand, South Africa, Singapore and the USA). They aim to help you transplant the games smoothly into your environment and run enhanced courses – not just carbon copies of courses from another environment or location.

We suggest that you do not have to reproduce all methods. Our experiences internationally indicate that the best approach to using the activities and dramaturgy is to add value to existing programmes and local activities. This means that you start with a local course design, update its structure using the dramaturgy approach and add games (probably somewhat modified) to enhance the course. This way, the course will reflect local needs, will use the strength of local traditions and can be reproduced in the future.

TEAM CONSIDERATIONS

The team approach is used to some extent by many experiential learning organisations around the world. The courses are run by instructor teams often composed of a chief instructor (sometimes with a deputy chief), group instructors, support instructors and various logistics staff. For purposes of running enhanced courses, you can use the teams in a variety of ways:

- Team with one instructor skilled in dramaturgy methods: Even if there is only one instructor in the team with knowledge of dramaturgy and games, you can still enhance your course. It will be mainly the instructor's responsibility to design the course. The other instructors do not necessarily have to be trained in the art of dramaturgy or games; they just need to know what to do and when, what to prepare, and what the basic idea is behind the special activities on the course.
- One-course team: A solution that is more time-intense in the short term, but more rewarding in the long term, is working in teams with different skills. One possibility is to set up a team that is designing, preparing and then running a course. Although the course design may take some time when done this way, the whole team will have bought into the idea of the course. Afterwards, they will be able to train other staff members to replicate the course (possibly with some modifications).
- Multiple-course team: The team can also be dedicated to running a particular course in several replications – or on a regular basis for any period of time – without any major changes in its composition. This repetition has the advantage of not having to train new staff; the downside is that the course then becomes greatly dependent on the skills and experience of specific people, and the gained experience may be difficult to transfer to others.
- Network: There can be several teams running different types of enhanced courses. The staff of these teams have similar skills and therefore they can participate on a variety of courses. You can select these staff for running practically any course.
- Centre-based vs. mobile team: While the activities have been originally prepared for teams that work together at the same location (the course centre), many of the activities can be

used in mobile teams (that is, teams in which members operate at various locations – course base, field, activity locations and so on). In this case, it is very important to agree on the activity responsibilities beforehand, thus limiting communication problems once the team becomes mobile.

PARTICIPANT CONSIDERATIONS

The courses described in this book are usually run for a group of 20–30 participants at one centre. However, with a bit of creativity, you can run the games and courses in other configurations as well.

- Bringing groups together: In a dislocated team it often happens that several smaller groups are in the field working independently with one or two instructors. It is often successful to bring several of the groups together for a larger game or course project, run by the team of the base staff or a joint game team composed of the field staff.
- Working in independent groups: Some games can be run successfully with a group of approximately 10–14 participants plus one instructor, but mainly those requiring less preparation.
- Group based at a centre: In some organisations, the course may be run at a base, where instructors work and live and other courses may be running concurrently. Our experience shows that even this situation does not present a barrier. While you have to make sure that the special time/space of your course does not interfere with the time/space of the base (and vice versa), you can use the resources of the base for your benefit. For example, in the case of a game needing many staff (see *Labyrinth*), you can invite other instructors to participate as external helpers.
- Participant acceptance and expectations: Another option is to organise games for unprepared participants. Depending on your organisation's image, participants sign up for a course with a certain expectation of its activities. Make sure that in your promotion of the enhanced course, you state clearly that the participants will encounter games, workshops, simulations, role-play activities, arts and discussions – simply anything that goes beyond the understanding of a standard course offered by your organisation.

GAME PREPARATION

While many of the games can be prepared and run by only one instructor, others need to be organised and run through a team approach. If you plan to have games requiring several staff members, the following hints may be helpful:

- Game knowledge: Not every instructor needs to be skilled in the art of the games, but it is necessary that one person briefs the rest of the staff.
- Division of roles: Make sure staff know their role during the game and do not go outside their knowledge limitation, as this can impair the whole game process.
- Staff creativity: You can create the special course and game atmosphere or modify it even if you have never taken a course on drama, painting or arts. Most of the games present a framework that will allow participants to express their creativity even without the instructors being experts in this creative area.

RUNNING THE GAMES

Key factors in running the games in other environments are:

- Modify games to reflect your course needs, staff availability, course environment, participant group and material available: The modification – following some general hints presented above – does not have to be very complex, yet can preserve or even enhance the spirit of the game for your own needs.
- All games can be modified to some extent: It may be a simple modification such as changing the framing of a game, but it can also be quite complex, such as adding new rules, or updating the game for a different number of participants. Given the nature of games, they are never cast in stone and simply need to be run in a way that reflects what you hope to achieve, not what the game is about. A new context may need a completely different approach to the game.
- Preparation time: While you always have to spend time planning, you can modify any game so it is logistically easier to run, and even a minimal form can be powerful.
- Material needed: Some games need special material, such as art equipment, special rule sets, tokens or other game elements, and so on. Make sure that you have all necessary material available well in advance, especially as in some remote outdoor centres they may not be easy to get. On expeditions you should take the minimum, so it is important to plan with logistics staff either to bring the material to the location or modify the game to use very little.

UTILISATION OF EXISTING PROGRAMME ELEMENTS

1492 – The Conquest of the Paradise was a game developed and created for a school course in Outward Bound South Africa. It ran for two days and only used what was at base HQ plus minimal extras (a drawing activity and atmospheric elements) to transport the participants back to fifteenth-century Spain. The game had a fantasy setting, strong motivation and an holistic approach to the in-game activities, combined with OBSA outdoor activities and facilities available on the base. The game was prepared in one day by one instructor experienced in such games. It was actually run with a team of local instructors, many of whom had not experienced such games before, but with a proper staff briefing, the game was a big success.

New games should not and do not have to replace your existing programme ideas; they can enhance and add value to your programmes! You may be surprised how many of your existing activities and facilities can actually be incorporated into the games – and vice versa. A common concern is that using the new games and course approaches will under-utilise the existing natural resources and outdoor environment. However, games run in wilderness/outdoor locations can be enhanced beyond their original setting. Do not feel limited by the environment description of the games and use what you have!

RUNNING GAMES ON EXPEDITIONS

Many of the games use the atmosphere of an indoor centre, but our experience indicates that, with slight modifications, some activities provide very positive results if their indoor potential is combined with the beauty of the outdoors in an expedition setting. A more important consideration is the overall dramaturgy of an expedition-based course. The expedition as such fills most of the slots otherwise available for games. However, what has worked well is a dramaturgy in which the expedition is still the primary method, but enhanced by the addition of several games. Another successful idea is a combined course, which uses a centre-based approach (with the main focus on games and expedition preparation) and an expedition (with the main focus on the expedition and adding games).

DISADVANTAGES OF A TEAM APPROACH

Whilst we have highlighted the many positive aspects of dramaturgy and a team approach to course design, the following disadvantages have also been identified:

- Low involvement: Instructors preparing another activity away from the participant group may lose track of the group dynamics development. It is important that they attend the activity review and that the daily team review provides a detailed description of the group dynamics.
- Mixing up roles: Participants may confuse the different instructors' roles (game chief, logistical support or even participants).
- Team stress: The team members must be able to co-operate under stress and tiredness. The potential emotional demands due to the diverse nature of the activities may also place extra pressure on staff. The volunteer instructors work long hours facilitating the courses and need time off after an intense course of this nature if burnout is to be avoided.
- The high level of preparation and number of instructors: The courses need to be modified for professional development programmes (PDP) into three- to four-day versions to be successful commercially.

Application of methods to PDP design

A specific area for application of experiential programmes is for company teams – 'Professional Development Programmes' (PDP). Whilst this area of training is well established in Britain and the USA, in the Czech Republic this way of team training, co-operation and developing leadership was practically unknown until the early 1990s. The change from a socialist regime, and new company environments, opened the door to management development and better understanding of the terms 'teambuilding' and 'leadership'. The logical pioneer was Outward Bound (Česká cesta), which was established at the beginning of 1993. Its target was to offer a new programme of professional development for managers and whole teams to the Czech market, and also to use the profit from these commercial courses for the development of the volunteer-staffed open-enrolment programmes. It was not just a simple case of replicating programmes from abroad, but a creative combination using dramaturgy principles, of traditional activities (icebreakers, dynamics, ropes courses, rock-climbing), with all sorts of games (strategic, dramatic) and creative workshops, which created an original product. There are three main types of programmes offered:

1 Management training
   - Usually for groups of 12–20 people.
   - Length two to four days.
   - General focus: teambuilding, teamwork, leadership, creativity and communication.
   - Specified focus in addition to classical improvements of team co-operation: preparation for change management, support of horizontal communication of middle managers, training delegation. A common combination is skills training, team process improvement and personal development.
   - Usually a four-member team of instructors/trainers with different levels of experience – very experienced chief trainer, senior trainer, junior trainer and assistant.
   - 9–12 programme hours per day.
   - Most of the activities are followed by group review where trainers play the role of discussion facilitators. They summarise the groups' thoughts and quite often compare these with theoretical models. The quality of the mediation between the experiential training activity and management training practice is essential.
   - After the course ends, the chief trainer puts together a final report, which contains comments on the course, characteristics of the group related to the tasks and also ideas for future team development.
2 Management assessment
   These courses assess management group processes as well as managers' personalities. These programmes are similar to management training but have a few specific differences:
   - Every employee must know that they will be observed during the programme. They will be reviewed at the end (usually by interview).
   - Groups are smaller, up to 16 people.
   - As well as trainers, there are specialists (psychologists, educational consultants) present who assess the participants in specific dimensions of behaviour on a chosen scale.
   - Standard psychometric and sociometric tests are added to the programme.
3 Team spirit
   Mainly fun programmes with a main target of creating informal social interactions, close personal contacts and team (company) spirit using interesting activities. Usually these programmes are aimed at developing networking at company meetings. They are often used as a reward, and help to build an informal creative atmosphere at the beginning of strategic meetings, or as part of social company happenings, sometimes including employees' partners. The characteristics are:
   - Varied group from 6–200 people.
   - Selection of activities related to targets – fun interactive games, adrenaline sports, variety of small competitions and creative workshops.
   - Spontaneous impact of experience; very rarely is there a group review.
   - Usually in combination with a social event – barbecue, sports tournament, and so on.

Although these are three relatively different products their preparation and realisation has the following common parts:

- A wider range of activities: Released from the confines of the outdoors, a wider range of activities (for example, arts and drama) are available as experiential tools, helping to reintroduce the element of the unexpected, which once featured strongly in management development programmes. Similar to open-enrolment courses, a scenario is prepared following the spirit of dramaturgy principles.

- The tailor-making approach: Programmes offer a much more flexible and energised approach for trainers and, for participants, the benefit of programmes aimed exclusively at them. Meetings with the client before each course identify the real needs of the client and refine programme targets, which are agreed by both sides. This tailor-made concept often creates original courses. During the programme trainers assess the actual development of the group dynamics as well as the new dimensions that each group generates during the course. Trainers are always ready to adapt the programme if they see it will maximise the benefits of the course.
- Self-development: Programmes are focused on self-development. In particular, the surreal nature of some of the exercises aims to broaden and open the mind. This surrealism neatly avoids the trap of 'isomorphic framing', meaning 'having the same structure' (Bacon, 1983). In isomorphic framing, a trainer addresses the briefing in terms of the similarities between the adventure and the corresponding present life experiences of the participants. Krouwel (2000) indicated that it was important for the participants to form their own isomorphic metaphors rather than have them externally imposed. One does not need to pretend that a rope spider's web is a distribution network. The skill is to make these highly powerful exercises act as a blank sheet on which delegates expose their true selves, allowing access to self-examination and the counsel of others.

Figure 5.1 identifies the steps and procedures used on PDP courses and the perceived benefits. The techniques have been developed from the public open-enrolment courses. Krouwel (2000) concluded that these techniques and the range of activities would benefit professional development practice in the UK, which had forgotten its idealistic roots. The ability to learn specified sets of behaviours only equips managers with the ability to deal with the immediate demands of their current (and maybe next) job. Provoking the imagination may well be infinitely more useful, helping them to think (and see) for themselves, not simply to behave as they have been programmed. This may help managers to see further than the distracting assistance of competencies, catchphrases and mission statements and help them to a greater self-awareness.

DIFFERENCES BETWEEN OPEN-ENROLMENT COURSES AND PDP

PDP courses typically involve teams of three or four trainers. The preparation time is considerably shorter than for longer programmes and seldom includes new activities. Once again each course is unique and the flexibility remains. Courses are typically two to four days, which makes the development of a full-scale dramaturgy difficult, often resulting in them following an activity/review cycle. However, the basic dramaturgy principles can be applied even to a four-hour workshop. The trainers are constrained by the short time period and how best to review these courses. They are keen to blend the dramaturgy methodology with traditional PDP practice, but without losing the distinctive innovative and creative approach. The relationship between the two is symbiotic, with the focus of debate being how to keep the essence of the dramaturgy methods, while translating them into a management context and also including more focused reviews.

Whilst after open-enrolment courses participants do not have to meet again unless they want to, the participants on company courses often meet the following working day in the

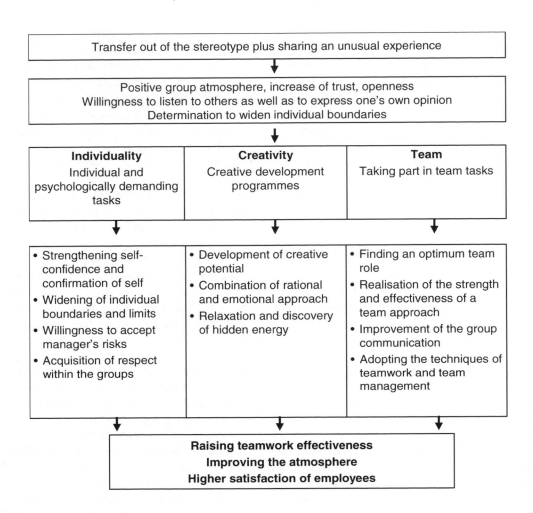

Figure 5.1   Techniques used during PDP courses and their benefits

same group and in the same working environment. This reality leads us to be careful when addressing sensitive topics. The selection of items and how open the discussion is must be decided by the group. Insensitive behaviour by a trainer can lead to major long-term problems for individuals as well as for the whole group.

Participants on open-enrolment courses freely choose to come and usually understand that they are investing in their own future and personal development. PDP participants are often there because of the decisions of their company leaders, so they may come to the course with different motivations. At the beginning trainers may have to persuade participants of its benefits, and encourage them to participate. A good way to achieve this participation is a combination of rational explanation, emotional charm and the high personal input of the trainers!

Initially we were afraid to include activities creating a lot of personal discomfort (for example, traversing a river, night activities) or unusual activities (painting techniques, drama). However, from our experiences we have learned that if such activities are not too bizarre and are presented in a meaningful way, the clients (including higher management) will find sense in them, do not mind the potential discomfort, and do not reject the programmes. On the contrary, quite often they applaud the difficulties, deepness and originality. Some of the activities (see Part 3), which are in their original format (or with moderate modification), are used on management development courses; for example, *Triffids*, *Camel Trophy*, *Las Vegas*, *Colour Mass*, *Pointillism* and *Wag the Dog*.

Figures 5.2 and 5.3 illustrate scenarios for PDP programmes that have been developed internationally. The 'Action Learning Management Programme' (ALMP) is a third-year university management development programme in New Zealand.

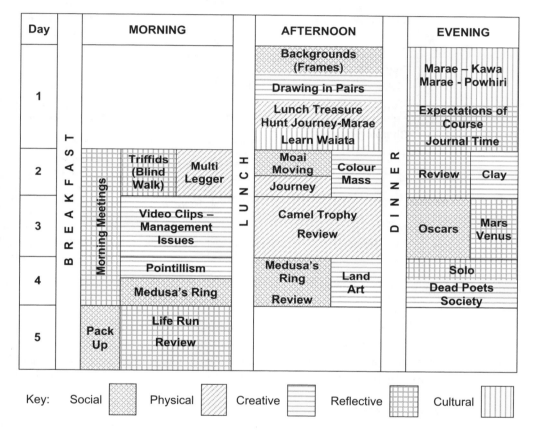

Figure 5.2   Action Learning Management Practicum 2002

The following is a brief description of some of the activities illustrated in Figures 5.2 and 5.3 (other activities are described in Part 3):

- *Backgrounds (Frames)* – an icebreaker activity, where participants introduce themselves through picture frames.
- *Drawing in Pairs* – a creative activity, where participants have a conversation through drawing without talking.
- *Blind Walk* – based on *Triffids*, participants walk blindfolded through a series of obstacles.
- *Multi-Legger* – a fun team running game.

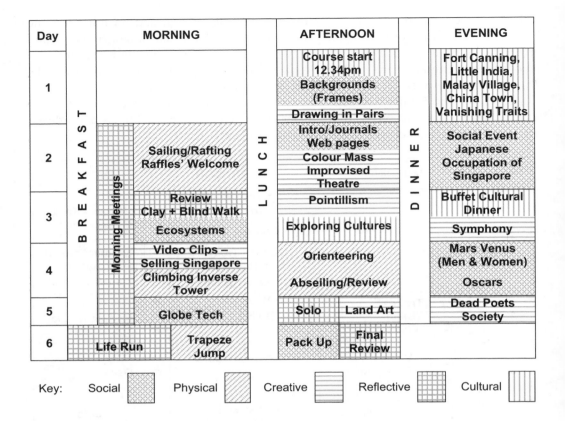

Figure 5.3   Singatouch 2003

- *Moai Moving* – a team strategy game based on the statues of Easter Island.
- *Clay* – a creative activity, involving exploring shapes with clay.
- *Video Clips* – a creative activity, based on *Wag the Dog*, where teams create video clips of themes (Management Issues, Selling Singapore), with an 'Oscar' award ceremony in the evening.
- *Medusa's Ring* – a team strategy activity.
- *Globe Tech* – a team strategy activity resulting in the construction of a raft.
- *Life Run* – an extended psychological activity that combines aerobic exercise with reflection, decision-making processes and the opportunity for application and integration of individual learning and insights.

The following is a quote from a participant illustrating metaphors related to the holistic impact of the ALMP:

The metaphor of a beach being composed of many separate parts relates to the ALMP program, which also is composed of many separate elements... with themes around creativity, teaming, personal reflection, and group discussions, with the outcomes of the program being influenced by these themes. The relevance of this to managers and the workplace revolves around the importance of balance, and ensuring we have time for 'whole-brain' activities, as well as those that appeal to our own specific learning styles. Personally I found the program was impact-full for my heart as well as my head... Distance provides a useful perspective, a bit like looking at a beach from the vantage point of a cliff top – certain things come to light that might not be apparent when on the beach itself. The importance of integration only really came to light after I left the program, and I became aware of greater levels of creativity, better thought processing and problem solving, as well as a sense of 'wholeness'. The impact of this on my work environment was that I felt more productive and better able to deal with the demands of my job.

Singatouch (meaning touching Singapore, not singing!) is a management development programme for educators created by Outward Bound Singapore. *Singatouch* aimed at building strong bonds among ethnic groups through a combination of role-play, creative, outdoor adventure and teambuilding activities. A national newspaper in Singapore described it as 'Artward Bound'!

6 *Using Games in the Programme*

It was like a lifetime of experiences/lessons compressed into two weeks. I knew that during this journey of two weeks I was learning what would possibly take me two years or more in my 'normal' life.
International course participant

Chapter overview

The main aim of this chapter is to enable you to run games presented in this book. Specifically, you will learn about:

- various types of games (examples are described in Part 3)
- fitting games into your courses
- preparation for a game.

What is a game?

There are many games that can be used, but the aim is to select those best suited for your particular course. In order to do this selection you need to know what effect a game can have on your programme.

UNDERSTANDING GAMES

A game is often said to be 'life as if' or 'a draft for life'. Games create a model world, allowing people to enter various life situations that are otherwise not accessed by them, to experiment with various situations or roles and to explore their reactions to new situations. More specifically the games presented in this book:

- aim to have a certain effect on people who are involved in them as players
- take place in a special environment
- use a special set of rules
- do not provide any material benefits to winners
- are usually framed or introduced in a fantasy setting, seemingly distant from daily life
- involve a group of human players who interact together and with the environment.

What makes a game connect to normality is the fact that the emotions, processes and interactions during a game are real. The game provides a fantasy environment, but the acting-out is real with a resulting impact on the participants. The stronger the reality of the in-game processes, the stronger is the resulting effect on participants. As Holcová (translated from Prázdninová Škola Lipnice, 1990, p.56) states:

> *The game isn't about communicating some information or teaching, but about an offer. 'See what it does so you're prepared for it when it comes for real.' The games awaken emotions, emotions mobilise energy and the need to invest energy leads the participants to discover themselves.*

GAME ELEMENTS

- Challenge: A game often requires participants to use resources and approaches that are challenging and that they do not normally use. The challenge can come on many levels: social, physical, creative, psychological, reflective, intellectual, emotional or even spiritual. The challenge element is closely related to the intensity of the game, which should be stimulating for the participants.
- Attraction: Every game must be appealing to the participants. Introducing the game using motivation can help in creating some of this attraction.
- Rules: Every game, even the least structured one, is defined by a set of rules.
- Appropriate audience: Many games have complex rules, take place in difficult environments, and require a range of skills. The complexity of some games, or the fact that the players need real life experience, may make them unsuitable for children.
- Special time/space: Every game has a defined time and space in which it takes place, although the space may be unusual and the time may flow differently.
- Physical, psychological and emotional safety: The concept of safety also relates to the fact that the participants are encouraged to explore the problematic parts of their own

performance and see them as learning opportunities, rather than as reasons to develop a negative self-image.

The scope of activities fitting these criteria is very wide indeed – a 'game' as we present it in this book can be anything from a team running competition to an improvisational theatre role-play evening almost without any rules...

Role of games

Every game can serve several functions. Keep in mind that a game is a means to an end, not the goal. A good game not only involves the participants and is a source of fun (and many other emotions), but also aims to develop certain attributes in themselves or the participant group. The main functions of a game are listed below.

GETTING OUT OF FAMILIAR ENVIRONMENTS

A game takes participants to an unusual world, with which they have very little familiarity. A game should create a special environment. Game participants become visitors to a new country – they have to adapt, learn the language of the new environment and find their way around. This adaptation may not be possible if they stayed in their home territory or comfort zone. In more traditional outdoor development courses, taking people to outdoor settings, often away from civilisation, fulfils this function. However, you can also meet this need by creating a special social, physical, creative or reflective atmosphere into which games are brought. Sometimes even a special course time is invented – days often have different rhythms from regular life, activities take place at unusual times and have different durations. However, the special time/space has to be created with caution and it should not be so unusual for participants that it removes them way too far from their comfort zone.

EXTENDING PERSONAL BOUNDARIES AND EXPLORING SELF

In the special world and time created by the game, participants often do things they did not know they would have to do or that they thought they actually could not do. They have to react to new stimuli and have a chance to explore aspects of themselves they do not normally see. If a game does not require any new skill or approach, it is not perceived as challenging enough, and adult players especially may not fully participate.

EXPLORING SOCIAL INTERACTION AND PLAY

Because social communication takes place during the majority of games, they can be seen as a playground for acting out various interactions and evaluating reactions. The games allow participants to play. Priest and Gass (1997) indicated that this play stage, or exploration and experimentation stage, of the adventure experience was important in developing 'peak experiences' and a 'state of flow'. Fun and play are also important in removing social barriers and stress, and increasing intrinsic motivation and relaxation. This importance is reinforced during activities which involve psychological and/or perceived physical risk, and which push participants to extend their comfort zone.

DEVELOPMENT OF SKILLS

- Social skills: Communication, trust, relating to people, leadership, empathy, teamwork and many other social skills are an essential part of many games.
- Intellectual skills: Participants are required to use logical thinking and analytical abilities, but also perception and strategy.
- Creative skills: Creativity involves not just art activity (painting, sculpting or crafts), but developing creative skills. Imagination and thinking 'out of the box' also takes place whilst problem solving.
- Emotional skills: All games result in some emotional reaction by participants, which can be of different intensity. As a result of specific games, participants may be able to explore their emotional world, express feelings normally repressed or discover their own emotional reactions. Other games may focus on developing self-efficacy, dealing with self-images and mindsets and challenging stereotypes.
- Physical skills: Physical activities not only help those involved to become fitter, but participants often voluntarily involve and accept many physical challenges they would not do otherwise.

Types of games

There are several game criteria:

Environment

- Outdoor games: Games can be run in wilderness settings as well as in the country.
- Indoor games: Many games are designed specifically for indoor settings.
- Games in urban environments: Several games could be modified for use in a large city or small country town.

Rules

- Highly structured games: These are games with a definite, complete and exact set of rules, which must be followed (see *Ecosystems*).
- Less structured and unstructured games: These are outlined in the introduction/ motivation and then the participants, with some instructor input (see *Dance Hall* or *Auntie Amalda*), embellish and expand the game. Instructors set the atmosphere (physical and social), framing and basic story of the game. Participants then have responsibility for decision, planning, action and creativity (see *Labyrinth*), or they may be given very few clues about the game world and have to react spontaneously (see *Poseidon*). These activities allow co-operation in difficult situations, flexibility, fast decisions, teamwork, adaptability and spontaneous creativity. Very seldom are they competitions – you can think of them almost as a performance.

Aims

The aim of a particular game is primarily dependent on its place in the overall course dramaturgy, framing, set-up of the game and the developing group dynamics. A specific game may appear as physical on one course and as social on another. However, none of the games fits into one clear-cut category – and most of them use social, physical, creative and reflective/emotional elements, with perhaps one (or more) aspect emphasised over the others. The following are the most common game forms (partly based on a classification by Hanuš, cited in Hrkal and Hanuš, 1998).

STAGED GAMES

These games require participants to face situations in which they compete against themselves. Such games represent the core activities encountered by participants on VSL courses. The aim of the game is not to solve a specific task, but rather to explore the process of solving the task and the impact that has on the participant. Various creativity-based games may also fall into this category. An example would be *Games without Borders*, which has no goal to accomplish or task to solve, yet it allows participants to enter many unusual situations and presents a challenge on a personal, emotional and social level.

TEAM AND STRATEGIC GAMES

These activities address issues such as leadership, passing information, dividing roles, taking responsibility, time management, planning and communication. On the base level it can bring physical, intellectual, and social challenge for individuals and trust amongst the group. Team games involving physical activity can also be quite competitive. The competition element can help motivation, increase effort, set atmosphere and create real conditions. Participants should feel that the game is not just about winning or losing – other aspects such as communication, support, honesty and general teamwork should be explored (Petrová *et al.*, 1999).

SIMULATION GAMES

A simulated environment and atmosphere allows participation in specific social roles. The role develops skills that can be used to approach a similar situation later in the real world. The role is not acting, but rather a potential social role of the participant. More complex games can use a competitive element. Very often, the line between team and simulation games is blurred. *Princess Shin-Sho* is a complex strategy game using teams competing against each other, simulating a complex project. The game requires full physical and intellectual involvement of the participants and has a winner.

INITIATIVE GAMES

These games involve a clearly defined physical or intellectual task for a team or an individual. Various icebreakers and energisers belong to this category as well. *Camel Trophy* is a physical team activity, which includes various smaller, or bigger, initiative games using the framing of an off-road four-wheel-drive rally.

ROLE-BASED GAMES

Often considered a sub-group of staged games, these activities are based on social interaction that constructs a certain set of events. The participants voluntarily take on various roles and collectively develop them. The roles the participants act are either identical to their personalities, just enhanced with new attributes needed in the special game world (simulation type of drama-based games), fictional (role-play type) or they refer to an existing person (characterisation type). All these types can be included in one game. Some of the major drama-based games need some participant preparation in the form of smaller games that introduce concepts of role-playing to them and also relax them so they can accept acting in public. Often the roles are assigned by instructors, specifically or randomly, to participants. Horáková (quoted in Petrová *et al.*, 1999, p.17) highlights an important related concern:

[When using a role-play game], you should know the participant group rather well. If people are playing roles that they like, the game can run smoothly and it can have really good atmosphere. If it is too challenging for most people in the group and they are not able to play or express their roles, it can influence the whole game. It is better not to challenge everybody at the same time [with roles they may struggle with], so they can help each other with their roles. For example, if all introverts become extroverts and extroverts become quiet and shy, it can happen that the game will be very quiet and without any action.

Dance Hall is an example of a role-playing game, in which participants act out a whole range of situations with the background of a dance activity. These activities provide participants with the opportunity/challenge to accept a role and become a new character, a chance to try something or be someone else. The role-play games may be eye-opening to participants. By trying a role not normally taken in real life, they may realise the part actually fits them and they adapt it when they return to their normal lives.

PSYCHOLOGICAL/REFLECTIVE GAMES

These games place a higher emotional demand on participants. These activities may lead to expressing emotions, exploring deep aspects of one's identity or acting out behaviours. They can also become an improvised theatre, and need to be supervised by instructors skilled in psychological or therapeutic work. *Labyrinth* is one of the most intense psychological games. Participants are encouraged to explore their present destiny or to create an alternate life plan and see its outcomes. They witness the death of their parents and eventually their own death; see their in-game children grow and face other major positive and negative life events – all during about five to six hours of game play. This game needs extremely sensitive and careful running.

SOCIODRAMA GAMES

Sociodrama involves acting out roles and usually takes place in a controlled discussion: it can focus on any issue of significance to the participant group. Sociodrama usually brings out strong moral and ethical values and the participants need to feel emotionally safe, therefore it should not be run at the beginning of the course. *Mars Venus* is a game that, using only discussions, allows participants to explore often surprising elements of their real lives.

PRE-COURSE GAMES

You can involve the participants weeks or even months before the beginning of the course. It is not uncommon to prepare a game for the participants that they may play together with other participants without being at the same physical location. Examples include asking participants to eat only combinations of foods they never tried before for a period of three days; performing a certain activity at a given time once a week for a whole month; and creating something and bringing it for use on the course. These pre-course games serve as a sort of motivation and encourage quicker community spirit amongst the participants on the course.

COMBINED FORMS

- Openings: These are often complex and production-intense projects, involving many special activities, which aim to bring the participants into the fantasy world on the first day of the course. These openings are usually planned weeks in advance and consume a very significant portion of the course planning time as well as instructors' energy at the beginning of the course. However, their function is critical and the planning time is necessary. The *Intertouch 2002* course initially gathered the participants together in Prague. There they met a character called Pilgrim, who sent them on a journey through the medieval city, where they solved several tasks and met other characters. They then rejoined Pilgrim who took them by bus to a castle in the country where the participants had dinner, followed by a fantasy tour through the castle which ended up with them creating their own 'coats of arms' (a self-presentation activity using fictional nobility coats). When night fell, instructors (dressed up as monks with torches) took groups of participants on a journey of several kilometres through the forest, during which they shared some of their personal values. Late at night, the groups gathered at the mansion that was to be the course centre for the next few days. There another instructor waited with a barn dance show prepared for the participants. When they woke the next morning, they all felt they had been together for much longer than one day...
- Closings: The closing activities' aims are similar to the opening – to prepare participants for new experiences and for a transition – only this time, back from the course world to daily life. At *Intertouch 2002*, after the various closing activities, just before the participants were about to leave the centre, Pilgrim showed up again and invited them to go on the next journey. He also introduced a creative activity, which was followed by a goodbye game that allowed the participants to part in an intense yet final way.
- Games in the background: Several games can be run simultaneously. They can be simple such as participants asking to do a good deed anonymously within the next few days. However, they can be also more intense and complex, as is the case of the *War of the Roses* game.

Although the following happen less often during courses, their effect may bring a desired result and, in an appropriate dramaturgy, they certainly have their place:

- Paradoxical games: These are activities aiming to break up the stereotype of games in the later stages of the course. The participants play a game defying all principles, which reminds them that nothing should be taken for granted on the course. Some of these activities have strong positive effects. For example, in the *Pinecones* game participants are divided into two groups, brought to a forest path, and given one hour to bring the cones from the right side to the left and from the left side to the right. The only introduction/motivation to the game is the quote 'sense begins where purpose ends'. Another *Pinecone*-type game involves an attempt to cover a small cottage with the cones in a given time limit (which of course is not long enough to cover even the base of the cottage).

- Tournament or competition: The task is to achieve a certain goal following rules of a specific sport. Competitions are used on the courses from time to time with a positive effect. The main aim is not to build competitive and individualistic orientation in the participants, but simply to provide an element of motivation to the game. The competitive aspect of some of the activities also comes from the need to have a contrast in the dramaturgy – a scenario without a competitive game would certainly miss something.

FORMS OTHER THAN GAMES

The courses consist not only of games. In fact, there may be areas in the course scenarios spanning several days, during which not a single game takes place. Very often, games are combined with other activities and although this book does not provide specific descriptions of these, they are worthy of note:

- Atmosphere activities: The special atmosphere on the course is achieved by a combination of any and all methods and tools the instructors have. This may be through games, activities, set-up of the centre, rituals, happenings and anything else you can think of that can create a special atmosphere. An example of an activity helping to create an atmosphere/ambience may be the setting up of lit torches in the forest during a walk to or from an activity in the night.
- 'Red threads': These are a series of small activities or rituals that flow through the whole course. For example, these can be regularly repeated discussions on various topics, or smaller activities performed by the participants (such as *Touches of the Nations*, where international course participants present something connected to their home country interactively – every day a different country). Essentially, they are activities that occur daily. The wake-up rituals, performed by instructors, may be related to the theme of the day, but in a very indirect symbolic way. A meal ritual may involve reciting a quote/poem. These threads occur regularly or daily and provide the glue that knits the course days together.
- Happening: The tradition of 'action art' street performances, or happenings, features strongly on most courses. An example could be face-painting followed by a dance simulating the life of an ancient tribe. Happenings may be seen as a form of a non-structured game. Be prepared for the fact that happenings may bring out very high energy and strong emotional reactions.
- Workshop, lecture or micro-course: Some of the course activities may introduce a new skill to the participant – for example, in the form of a hand-made paper workshop or an orienteering lesson. Workshops such as dance, drama, colour and music involve spontaneous creativity, discovery and trying new things. Creativity can be stimulated by requiring an unusual technical design or by solving a social situation, as well as by different ways of working in a team. If you use a workshop, the participants should be encouraged to make mistakes; the process is more important, not the result. Activities should graduate from easy steps to more difficult ones; ideally they should start with a warm-up,

introduction and allaying fears. The atmosphere (music), place and reflection times during the activity are also important (Petrová *et al.*, 1999).

- Audio/visual presentations: These are activities in which, for example, participants listen to a presentation about a trip to India, participate in a reading of French poetry, watch a movie on a large screen set up in a meadow, or listen to a CD with music related to another activity in the course. These activities require little participant input and can balance the course energy, giving participants time to relax. They may be followed by a related physically active game.
- Exhibitions and performances: A presentation of participants' creative efforts – this may take place within the course or in an external environment; for example, an artwork display, or a theatre performance in a local village or an old peoples' home. There was even a case when a photographic exhibition went on a year-long tour after the course finished!
- Expedition: One- to five-day expeditions, often including other activities and games, which focus more on exploration than physical challenge. These *turistika* expeditions involve tramping/hiking (or travelling by bike, train, and so on) through the countryside. They also involve cultural, environmental, service and local history activities, as well as interacting with local people.
- Inspirational guests: They could run an audio/visual presentation, a game or a combined activity, also be part of a whole set of activities culminating in a lecture, workshop or interview given. Traditionally the guests have been special and very often quite famous people, and in some cases, meeting them has been a highlight of the course. Examples include politicians, popular journalists, CEOs of large corporations, Olympic winners, refugee workers or famous artists.
- Outdoor adventure activities: A whole range of traditional outdoor activities plays an important role on most of the courses. The most common are rock-climbing and abseiling, but rafting, raft building, cycling, orienteering and many more may be used. They are good examples of activities that work on a game course, even when they are not presented as games; that is, you do not have to set up a fantasy environment for a rock-climbing session. On the other hand, if you manage to make an activity of this type part of a larger game, it adds a lot to the rhythm and variety of the game.
- Service activities: The time involved may range from a few hours to a whole day. For example, these may be activities that ask participants to help with daily chores at an old people's home, and bring back stories.
- Other activities: The range of activities is unlimited, and depends only on the creativity of the team and the overall course dramaturgy. Some common 'other activities' include, for example, sweat-lodge building; service at the centre; musical performances, or activities centred around the improvised tea room that many courses create at their centres; 'Wall of Laughs' and 'Wall of Cries' comprise sheets hanging on the centre's walls, available for anonymous messages, massages, meditations or visualisations.

Fitting the game into the scenario

DRAMATURGY CONSIDERATIONS

So how do you choose a game or other activity for a course and where should it be placed in the course dramaturgy and scenario? Essentially, most games can be run at any time, with any group, in any environment. However, the effects of the same activity will vary to a huge extent depending on the circumstances. An activity run in a certain context may have a totally different effect if held in an alternative environment. Make sure you do not plan a game isolated from the rest of the course!

The key question to selecting a specific game is: 'How do I fulfil the dramaturgy wave in a particular time of its development?' For example, you do not select a game to happen on the evening of Day 3 just because it is your favourite activity and there seems to be a free slot, but because it will help you achieve a particular dramaturgy need. The overall course goal or direction may alter during the course, and it is one of the greatest challenges of the practical dramaturgy (the dramaturgy on the course) to select new games and activities appropriate to constantly changing dramaturgy waves.

Once you know what type of activity may be appropriate for the dramaturgy, you can then consider several other key criteria to help in the selection of the best activity. These are considered below.

RHYTHM

Dramaturgy works with changes and contrasts of rhythm. The whole course is very intensive and it is important to keep the pace balanced between the energy levels of the participants and the team of instructors. Metaphorically speaking:

> We are able to see breaks in the raindrops. We don't see any drops in a flowing river. There is no rhythm in anything flowing.
>
> Cicero, translated from Knotek, 2001, p.14.

You are creating 'drops' with your games and activities on the course: there needs to be a contrast among them. Rhythm is one of the key elements of dramaturgy design. Therefore, you have to make sure you are not selecting a game of a type that has already been used on the course too many times, takes place in the same environment or is run by the same instructors. On a well-balanced course with a good rhythm, the fast and physically demanding games are alternated with more quiet or meditative activities presented by different instructors. You should also change the daily time schedules.

PARTICIPANT DEMOGRAPHICS

Another key issue is the demographics of the participant group. Young adults have different needs and approaches to games from seniors; an international group will react differently from a nationally homogenous group; all-male groups will approach a game differently from mixed groups and so on. Some games are inappropriate for certain groups and you always need to investigate:

- How well do people know each other already?
- What is the strength and level of the relationships in the group?
- What are the group dynamics at the moment the game starts?
- How physically fit are the participants (overall and at a given moment)?
- How mentally fit are the participants (overall and at a given moment)?
- What is the age composition of the group?
- What is the gender composition of the group?
- What is the cultural composition of the group?

USING THE ENVIRONMENT

Another important decision is in what environment you want to run the game. Many games can be run both indoors and outdoors, but some are specific to a certain geographical or indoor location. A key thing to consider is that a great setting can enhance a game, but a bad environment can destroy even the best one.

TIMING

At what time of the day do we want to run the game? A seemingly trivial game may have an incredibly powerful effect if run at night, or an intellectually demanding game could fade if run straight after lunch. You also have to make sure you have enough time – a 'Parkinson's Law' of game planning says 'No matter how much time you allocate, you will always need 25 per cent more.' Be generous with the time you give yourself for game preparation and running. One of the big difficulties is when you overrun the time, effectively cancelling the game that was supposed to start next. This situation can affect the overall course flow. Also, make sure you are not stealing sleeping time from the participants (or the team!), otherwise be ready to provide it during the next day.

Another important consideration is that the game is not introduced too early in the course. If the participants are not ready, that particular game could end up as a very shallow attempt. Similarly, some may be introduced too late in the course, as in the case of easy activities that will not be challenging enough for participants. A more serious situation, though, is the case of psychologically demanding activities. A rule in dramaturgy development is that all psychologically intense activities should ideally come no later than three days before the end of the course. This provides enough time to handle the participants' initial reactions to such games while they are still on the course.

ADAPTING THE GAME

You may have a few ideas for an activity, but realise that none of them fits one or more of the criteria for it. You can either create a new game or adapt a game. While creating new games is not discussed in this book, adaptation is usually all that is necessary to change an existing game to fit the requirement of the dramaturgy. However, be aware that you should not alter the key elements of the original game, and you should run through the new version, at least mentally, to make sure it will work. The easiest-to-do adaptations take place in the following areas:

- Motivation/atmosphere: Without many problems, you can often change the fantasy setting of the game to fit the overall course mood.
- Intensity: Some activities can be made less intense (psychologically, physically or otherwise) to make sure they fit the momentary level of participants. Changing the activity duration, running it during daytime, shortening the physical requirements, or making the introduction less involved can lessen the intensity.
- Number of participants: Many activities need to be adapted to reflect either too high or too low numbers of participants. This often involves just adding more sub-groups, but sometimes this may require changing the rules, which needs greater consideration.
- Timing/environment: Remember that if you run a game in a different time, duration or environment from the original, you may get totally different or unexpected results! Therefore, changing any of these parameters needs to be considered seriously.

7 *Game Logistics*

The critical element is that this experiment occurred in a cocoon of safety/support/ compassion/caring, allowing me to play full out.
International course participant

Chapter overview

Voilà! You have selected the game and included it in the scenario. If you have not run games before, it may help to consider them as projects. As in the case of any project, you have some time, people and resources available (everything in limited amounts and usually less than you wish); you have deadlines, milestones and even clients. Just the subject matter is different: you are not launching a software product, but a game. Although this chapter mostly applies to structured games, we will provide some basic hints about the logistics for less-structured and non-structured games as well. This chapter will explore how to:

- use your instructor resources for running a game
- introduce the game
- present the rules
- manage the game flow once it has started
- react to some more common problems during the game
- wrap up the game
- manage physical, psychological and other risks during the game.

Set-up

STAFFING

Before you start preparing the game, several decisions must be made. The first is staffing:

- Game chief: This person is the project manager of the game. Experience shows that having more than one game chief often results in mismanaged projects. The role of the game chief is to run the preparation, the game and the review; however, anything can be delegated to other team members. It should be noted that the game chief may be the least visible team member for the participants. Especially logistically difficult games require the chief to take a strict co-ordinator's role from headquarters and communicate with the team remotely. In less-structured games, the game chief is the *deus ex machina* – the boss of the game world who can decide on modifying it in any way during the game.
- Instructors for preparation: Most of the games require some time for preparation and often this is best done within the team of instructors. It helps the game if the preparing instructors are the ones that run the game later.
- Instructors for running the game: You may need instructors at checkpoints or working with sub-groups, plus instructors who take on various roles during role-play activities, or people who assist participants during a workshop, and so on. These are the leaders who are visible to the participants. However, some games also need logistical staff – people who prepare locations during the duration of the game, break down other locations, serve the field instructors with material they need, and so on. You may also need instructors who will serve as communicators between the staff if the game chief is not taking this role for whatever reason. For the less-structured games, the instructors may take roles of specifically briefed participants – they are characters who interact with the participants in a special way during the game.
- Expert staff: Qualified staff may be required for some outdoor and/or psychological games (see *Stalker*). In this case, external instructors may be invited to run them.
- Instructors for debrief: In most cases it is the game chief, supported by the game field staff, who makes a plan for the review and then facilitates it. Of course even this role can be delegated.

MATERIAL

Before you go into the field you need to make sure the game can be run with the resources (instructors, time for running, time for preparation and material) available. Sometimes the material preparation takes much more time and energy than you may expect, so make sure you plan the preparation well ahead. In particular, the less-structured games are dependent on how well you create the special game world and this task may be material-intense. You also have to prevent the situation whereby these resources become exhausted for other activities after running your game.

ENVIRONMENT- AND ATMOSPHERE-CREATING ELEMENTS

Some outdoor games may need several hours of preparation – setting up the tracks, making maps, delivering material to checkpoints, and so on. Sometimes the environment preparation needs to take place in phases – beginning with the basic set-up long before the activity and finishing by putting the (sometimes not cheap) material on track just before the beginning of the game.

Many games require a special atmosphere – this can be achieved by modifying the environment. Especially in the case of indoor programmes, you can transform a room into, for example, a cyberpunk factory, a Roman theatre or just a very colourful, soft-feeling place. Do not underestimate this part, as the atmosphere helps a great deal with participants accepting the situation and being motivated to enter into the game. The special atmosphere creation is usually the only, and the crucial, part of field preparation of less-structured and indoor games. Note the room may have been in use just prior to your activity so make sure you have enough time for preparation before the official start of your game.

LOGISTICAL PLAN AND TEAM BRIEFING

Many of the activities need quite detailed co-ordination of the team and sometimes the instructor co-operation on the team is quite complex. In some cases, even a written minute-by-minute schedule distributed to game staff is required to make sure everyone knows exactly what to do. No matter how well the game may have been prepared, if your staff do not know what is going on during the game, what to do or how to react in unexpected situations, the entire game may backfire. Sometimes the staff briefing may be reminiscent of a military briefing of fighter pilots before leaving for a mission. As a game chief, do not hesitate to take on an uncompromising general's role, as it is your responsibility to make sure everyone knows everything they need to know (which only rarely means they need to know everything), especially:

- when they enter the game
- what exactly their role is and how their role relates to other staff members
- the timing and sequence of key in-game events and the triggers for them
- the overall game structure and at least an overall overview of the rules
- the most likely developments of the game
- how much information they should give to the participants and to whom they will refer participants with questions
- the time when they exit the game, their role in the debrief and game clean-up.

They also need to be briefed on safety risks, evacuation routes and the most likely problematic situations happening during the game, with clear instructions what to do in each case. If the instructors have multiple roles in the game (for example, participating in the motivation and then being an instructor on a checkpoint), they need to be briefed for all roles separately and fully.

In the case of less-structured and role-play games, you also have to brief the staff on the roles they play, on the dramatic events they introduce in the game, and on the overall in-character behaviour you expect from the instructors during the role-play game. For example, in the case of the *Dance Hall* game, instructors may take on at least three or four different roles. The instructors must have an understanding of their character, the desired type of interactions and see their character in the big picture view of the overall programme.

Plan enough time for the briefing! Do not forget the question-and-answer session, and a time for overview and checking out that everyone understands what is happening.

Like any good project manager, you should also encourage your assisting instructors – especially if they are running a game for the first time, or if the game is complex. The stress on the team may be much greater than you had anticipated.

PARTICIPANTS' PREPARATION

As the activity is approaching, you need to prepare the participants. They usually learn about the game no longer than a couple hours before it takes place, sometimes just a few minutes, but this does not mean they should come unprepared for the game. Pay special attention to announcing what clothes they may need for the game, and be very specific, because when the participants do not know what game is coming up, they only have your guidance on wearing the right gear. Also, some of the active games need a good physical warm-up.

No matter how secret you want to be about the particular game, it is extremely important to check out with people who may have a potential problem with the game in advance. You may have to tell them exactly what the game is going to be about and let them make an informed decision about whether or not to participate. In the case of participants who may need special attention, you can create a role for them, whereby they can play the game, but possibly in a limited capacity. For example, a person who cannot run may be recording their group's score in the depot; or a person who feels that they are overloaded by the course intensity could take an observer's role during the activity, making a record for the group.

Some role-play games (such as *Dance Hall* or *Las Vegas*) need extra time for participant preparation. They are assigned a role and then given some time (an hour or so) to select an appropriate costume and prepare for their roles. They come for the beginning of the activity in character all dressed up and ready to start the game.

TYPES OF INTRODUCTION/MOTIVATION

Each game usually starts with an opening, which sets the atmosphere and tunes in the participants. It is what we call motivation and is connected with the theme of the game (...and possibly the theme of the course on a deeper level). The motivation is an engaging and interactive performance by the instructors that introduces the activity and sets the atmosphere before any technical details are explained. Motivation is not just framing, as it is known in more traditional outdoor programmes. Besides providing a frame for the game or activity, it also creates the special atmosphere of the fantasy game world. The motivations need careful planning and can take a lot of energy and thought on behalf of the instructor. Instructors who are empathetic, energetic, verbally skilled and have some role-play ability usually make the best motivators.

The complexity and intensity of motivation varies according to its position in the course dramaturgy. Usually, at the beginning of the course, the motivations are long, intense and full of various props. As the course progresses, the need for strong motivation decreases and by the end of the course, the participants usually need very little. Interestingly, motivation does not have to take place before an activity. It does wonders to participants' curiosity if you introduce a motivation for an activity at the end of the day (a theatrical skit, watching the film *Stalker* or reading a chapter from a book) and then send them to bed. The participants do not know if they are going to be woken up at night (they will be, in the case of *Stalker*), if the game will take place sometime during the next day or whether what they witnessed was the motivation for a game at all. Elements like these greatly enhance the mystery of the course and help generate even higher participant energy for the course activities.

Motivation is very powerful and will influence the way participants approach the entire game. For example, if you want to run a serious activity, make an appropriate, low-fun motivation.

Some of the most common forms of motivation are (see games in Part 3 for further examples):

- Theatrical act/skit: The instructors act out some dramatic piece – with costumes, roles and a special environment. The act may end up openly inviting the participants to follow… already in game mode.
- Listening or viewing the libretto: The libretto is a text – such as a story, dialogue, poem or documentary writing – that presents the story of the game. The libretto can be read; but it can be also screened if it is presented as part of a movie or slide show.
- A small activity: This may end up opening a gate to a larger activity; for example, groups may get a role dependent on the result of an icebreaker.
- Game explanation: There may be instances – for example, when you need to break up the stereotype of ways games are introduced – that the game mechanism and goal are explained in plain words, without any bells and whistles. You need to make sure before using this method that the participants have a high level of natural motivation to get involved in the activity.
- Written motivation: For example, the *Las Vegas* game needs to be introduced some time before the game takes place so the participants can prepare for their roles. Often it is done by a couple of instructors coming in the roles of casino owners to the dinner and handing out fancy written invitations to the casino opening. Participants learn all they need from this invitation.
- Minimal introduction: In other cases, you may want to tell as little about the game as possible (in this case, double-check you spoke with all the people who may have a potential issue in the game). This method leaves the participants with scope to use the full range of their imagination.

DIVISION INTO GROUPS

Before getting into the rules, you may want to divide participants into groups, should the game require it (and many games do). Here are the most common approaches:

- Random division: It does not have to be just plain drawing a virtual line between the participants: you can be more creative. For example, each participant draws a slip of coloured paper and the colours make up groups.
- By a certain skill: Divide groups in terms of skill sets. You can call out 'Who liked maths?' 'Who has ever painted a painting?' – and divide the people evenly by their responses.
- By a positive or negative social relationship: Some games require a group of people who have a good relationship, and others use the challenge of bringing together people with a negative social relationship. One of the most reliable ways to find positive and negative social relationships is simple socio-metrical research. You can ask participants to write

down the names of three participants they would and three they would not take to a deserted island. They also need to sign this paper. This information is very sensitive so you need to make sure participants understand you are keeping the results just for yourself and the team. Then you can either use the individual responses to verify that you are putting together groups that will fulfil the criteria you want, or you can make a table with a row and column for each participant and record the mutual preferences onto one sheet. This information will help you not only construct the groups, but also see your group's social stars and outsiders.

- By letting team captains choose the teams: Not only do you tend to get evenly balanced teams, but this is also a strong feedback activity. If you let the captains select the members of their teams in turns, there will always be outsiders who will be chosen last. A way to make this negative effect smaller is to nominate the outsiders to become captains. Be careful of the social and individual implications with this method.
- By how much they know each other: It usually makes the game more intense if you bring together people who do not know each other well. A popular dividing procedure on management courses is to ask participants to form couples (trios and so on) of their friends. Then, you let the couples or trios stand behind one another... resulting in forming two or three lines. The groups are then defined by the lines.
- Special participation: A few of the games use rather unusual but important ways of selecting participants for the activities. In some versions of the *Stalker* activity, it is the instructors who select only a few of the participants to take part in the game. The *In the Skin of John Malkovich* game lets participants sign up for the game well in advance. The participants who do not sign up have a special, non-game role. This method is sometimes chosen when you want to emphasise the voluntary nature of the game, or if you have a good reason to limit the numbers participating.

RULES

So, the motivation is finished and the participants are ready to go! Now, the key part of the introduction comes. If you do not do the 'Rules' part well, the entire game can turn into a nightmare for the instructors and confusion for the participants. When presenting the rules you definitely need to know them completely. If you have a slight doubt about them before the game, do not hesitate to postpone the start of the game until you have them clarified – a better choice than risking bad or conflicting rules.

Make sure you give participants enough time for studying the rules. How much is enough? It depends on the aim of the game and therefore on the dramaturgy. If you want to challenge the group in a strategy game, make the time for studying the rules a part of the game. If the team has only just started working together, ensure the members have plenty of time to understand the rules. Make sure everyone has a chance to get the rules. If you are presenting the rules orally, keep the group focused. Although it can be argued that it is the participants' fault if they do not pay attention, sometimes this learning experience is outweighed by the negative experience of totally confused participants during the game.

After you present the rules (using one of the methods mentioned below), it is useful to give participants time to study the rules, which will allow them to formulate questions for the Q&A session. Be aware that they may ask you about things they should get from the rules or things that are already part of the strategy, which is another reason for you to know the game well.

Do not forget, or underestimate, logistical or safety rules. You may have to step out of the game world for this part. Participants may be mentally already out there in the game universe and will not think in real world terms; but if, for example, you do not explain to them how to put the helmet on and in what situations, you are risking a hard landing on the real world ground for them. Preferably give the safety briefing before starting the game rules.

Depending on the game, its complexity and aims, you can choose the most appropriate way of presenting the rules:

- Central rule sheet: You can write the key parts or all of the rules on a large sheet of paper that is constantly in front of them. This is not very practical in the case of a large number of participants, but is easy to produce and guarantees everyone see the rules.
- Hand out rules: If you really want to make sure everyone has understood the rules – which may be the case in complex games (see *Ecosystems*), it is worth distributing a photocopy of the rules to each participant.
- Oral presentation: In some cases, you may want to make it more challenging and not give out any written instructions. The participants can train their listening and sharing skills, but be prepared for a big question-and-answer session and possible confusion during the game. To make it hard, you can forbid making notes.
- Completing the rules: Make getting the rules part of the game. This brings a stronger mystery setting, as the participants have no idea what is going on until they complete finding the rules (for example, in a scavenger hunt or simple orienteering course, with the rules on checkpoints, and so on). You have to make sure that all the rules can be collected in a relatively short time; you do not want to ruin a great game by participants not being able to find the rules.
- Little-structured games: The introduction/motivation gives hints about the kind of rules participants can make up for themselves. If it is a role-play activity you can hang up a sheet of paper listing the roles.

Finally, do not change any game rules (unless safety is compromised) once the game has started. For participants, interfering in this way can ruin the game and potentially later parts of the course.

Running the game

'3...2...1... Your time is running!' The game has started, or in case of less-structured games, you may have turned the music on and started observing how the participants create their game world. Surprisingly, the same game with different participants may take very different forms from what you imagined. Several key staffing considerations will ensure the game runs smoothly.

THE CO-ORDINATOR

The game chief is usually the game co-ordinator. Their role is to:

- check that the game is run according to the rules
- watch for or predict problematic developments

- ensure safety (physical, psychological, environment, material)
- ensure that the time frame is not extended.

In less- and free-structured games, the game chief mainly checks the dynamics, co-ordinates in-game events with staff, and is more like a director in an improvised theatre.

THE JUROR

Seldom used in less- and free-structured games, this role is usually fulfilled by the game chief. The juror is:

- The only person answering participants' questions concerning the rules (if there are instructors at checkpoints, they also need to know the rules, as the participants cannot run to the juror all the time).
- The ultimate arbiter with the final decision on rules in case there may be more than one interpretation of them (no set of rules is complex enough to count with participants' creativity in their interpretation!).
- The ultimate arbiter in conflict between participant groups. Another answer is to mediate the dispute after the game or let the entire participant group handle potential conflict.

GAME STAFF ROLE

As an instructor helping to run the game you have to:

- Make sure you are at the right place at the right time doing the right thing – have all necessary materials with you, plus the game logistics schedule.
- Communicate to the game co-ordinator any unexpected developments or safety concerns.
- Provide positive motivation to the participants if it is thought necessary by the game chief.
- Provide negative motivation to the participants if appropriate, but this needs to be done very sensitively and at the right time and place. Well-timed sentences like 'You're the worst group I've had in this game' or 'Gee you guys are lazy today' may mobilise some energy in the participants.

In less-structured and role-play games, the staff may have a dramatic role; that is, they play an in-game character that interacts with the participants in a special way. The instructors need to be well briefed about the character because they will never know how the participants will react, and will need to improvise their interactions.

INSTRUCTORS AS GAME PARTICIPANTS

As a way to break up the traditional instructor/participant view, instructors are often playing games together with the other participants. This participation allows a new level of relationship between participants and instructors, blurs the us-and-them thinking and also recharges the instructors' batteries. However the instructors should still remember their duties and responsibilities so the functional division between the group of instructors and participants is not compromised. If there are instructors who are neither running nor participating in the game, they have to make sure they do not interfere. As a participant-instructor in a game:

- Do not reveal any extra rules you know to the group.
- Do not compare your present group to previous ones.
- Do participate 100 per cent as if you were a participant (so no chatting with game staff, taking breaks, and so on).
- Do whatever you would as a participant regarding cheering up your group and do not stay back if you would not do that as a participant!

Game flow

As the game chief, you may encounter unexpected situations, but experience will help you overcome these and maintain the game flow.

SAFETY FIRST

If you feel that safety can be potentially compromised, you must stop the game, if necessary change the rules or cancel the game. Safety must take preference. Although most of the risk management is covered during the planning and setting up of the game, nevertheless you should check all safety requirements while the game is in progress. Risks need to be managed under:

- physical safety
- psychological and emotional safety.

Safety applies to participants, instructors and any other people who may be affected by the game. Second, safety also applies to:

- the environment
- the material being used.

For more ideas about how to manage some common risks, see the section in this chapter on 'Risk management'.

TIMING

What if the game needs more time than you expected? We do not mean when the participants fail to complete a task in their given time-frame, but rather the situation when you realise you gave too little time for accomplishing all the game stages. Possible solutions are:

- Stop the game even if the participants have seen only a little bit of it. Be prepared though that the overall effect will be different from that if the participants had completed the game.

- Extend the time. It is a very risky decision, and you should not make it without consulting with the game chief of the following activity and possibly the course chief instructor as well.
- Modify the game so the tasks are more appropriate for their time-frame, but be very careful about changing the rules.

What if you have prepared your game to run for a certain time and suddenly see that the participants are able to solve it in a very short time? Alas, there is not much you can do to make the rules more difficult during the running of the game without alienating the participants.

- You can repeat the game with some modification to the rules or handicaps to the participants.
- Do nothing and just move on to the next activity. The participants probably enjoyed winning your game easily, and at least some positive energy may have been generated.
- A usual mistake is for the instructors to raise 'what if' questions during the review of such a too easy game, mentioning the hypothetical situations they hoped to see during the game. This questioning just confuses participants.

Finally, what if the game was well planned logistically, but just happens to be too difficult and the participants struggle to get through the first stages? Time is running out and you know that they will not be able to finish the game.

- Modifying the rules to make it easier is possible, but there is a danger the participants will see you as soft and will rely on your intervention during following activities, which in turn could reduce their learning experiences and independence.
- You can let the game continue and then focus on the process during the review. As the participants have not fulfilled the task they may pay attention to an ideal model that would help them solve the game. Be careful though – if it is obvious that the game was too hard, the best choice is just to admit it; otherwise they will see you as wishing to let them down.

RULE CHANGES

What if you or the participants find a part of the rules that does not make sense? How do you react?

- You can stick to the rules, even if they are wrong. This is practical only if you are unable to communicate with the entire group.
- You can remove or modify the rule, but must then ensure every participant knows about the change.

Make sure the game is updated and that instructors (organisation-wide) have a chance to learn about the problem after the course.

What if various participant groups are given different rules? It is tempting not to do anything and hope that other groups will not find out about the easier rules. However, it is not ethical and presents a huge risk of lessening participant trust in the following activities. It can also ruin the game and generate some negative feelings among the participants towards other games or course staff. If you find this situation has happened, you can:

- Find which group has the easiest rules and modify the others' rules to reflect the easier regime (do not do it the other way round).
- If you cannot communicate the change in the rules to all groups, acknowledge your problem afterwards and focus on the process rather than on the goal.

During less-structured activities, which let the participants create their own game world including the rules, sometimes the game flow starts going in a direction you really do not like. It may not necessarily be negative. For example, the participants may enjoy the game so much they generate and expend incredible energy, but you may need some of this energy for later games. Another situation may arise when some participants become totally immersed in their character resulting in negative behaviour, which has a negative effect on the rest of the group. The game chief must intervene and preserve the emotional safety of participants.

AFTER THE GAME

When the game finishes, there are several things you have to do:

- Mark the clear end of the game: A weak ending can lower the participant energy generated by the game.
- Announce results (in case of competitive games): If possible, give the results on the spot (of course, you may have to do it later – that is, before the review time, if counting the results takes more time). Do not just announce the results, make a big show about it! You do not have to praise the winners too much; the show can be great for everyone if you focus on the process and on the accomplishment of all. However, do not downplay the role of the winners – after all, they expect to be announced and that is your role. Dr Allan Gintel states: 'On the course, every single participant needs to experience 15 minutes of fame – and 15 minutes of hell.' The post-game time is your opportunity to let this happen.
- Wrap up: Especially in the case of less-structured games, there are no winners or results to announce, but you must still have definite ways to end the game. You can use another skit by the instructors, make an exhibition of the game creations, or include a structured part at the end of the unstructured game (perhaps self-presentations of each of the participant's roles in the game).
- Quick staff debrief: As the game chief (or the person running the review if it is not you) you need to be briefed by the game staff about the way the game developed, key issues, approaches the participants took and any problems. This debrief needs to be quick, as you will use it in the review.
- Upcoming team update: The game chief, or a delegated person, needs to talk to the leader of the next game immediately after their activity ends. You need to advise on:
  - the actual state of the group dynamics
  - what were the main outcomes and learning in this game
  - what is the physical/emotional level of the group energy
  - if there have been any conflicts in the group
  - if there are some participants who need special attention.
  It is advisable for the game chief of the next game to observe the review of the previous activity.

- Clean up: One of the least popular instructor duties is to clean the environment and material used. The best time to do it is straight after the game. In some games the material collection can be made part of the game. For example, the participants may get a special bonus if they bring some material back from the checkpoints, or you can ask them to help you with the clean up immediately after the game. Often they will not mind, especially if the game ended on a high, as it gives them time to relax and enjoy some unstructured time together.
- Time off: Unless it is planned, do not rush participants into another activity. Participants may be physically tired, or their clothes may need changing. There are also emotions generated from the game that may need time to be absorbed by the individual. Without time off, you can bury the potential effect of the game. In the case of some high-intensity, reflective and psychological games, do not hesitate to give time off – even several hours without any activity. Make sure you keep an eye on participants who you feel may have taken the activity intensely on an emotional level, and do not hesitate to check in a gentle way to see if they are OK before leaving them on their own.
- Review: The review is an essential part of the courses, if perhaps sometimes done in an untraditional way. The basic aim of the review has been described elsewhere in this book.

Risk management

Careful planning and running of the games can prevent potential problematic areas. These can occur in the areas of safety, but you also want to avoid risks in the dramaturgy, and to the whole course. The activities usually have strong themes and care is needed to ensure the physical, emotional and psychological safety of the participants and also of the instructors. You should always follow all the safety rules of your organisation. The following points focus your attention on some special areas, but this is certainly not a complete list of all safety measures relating to the running of games.

OBSERVING PARTICIPANTS

During the game, look for signs in individual participants which hint that they may be getting out of their physical or emotional comfort levels:

- unusual behaviours (other than the participant normally demonstrates)
- physical exhaustion
- expressing emotions unusual for the particular participant
- unusual silence; being out of the game; being closed out
- tears
- loud, over-excited, aggressive or hysterical behaviour
- whole-group negative behaviours (group hysteria, groupthink, and so on).

You may need to intervene to prevent problems:

- If you feel things are getting too intense during the game, bring in another more senior instructor as an observer, step in to lessen the intensity or terminate the game. If you stop the activity, make sure it is not an abrupt ending and that you work with the current state of the group after you finish the activity!

- Decrease the intensity of the activity.
- Bring in a stop time or a timeout – five or more minutes totally out of the game, in which the participants return to the real world.
- Check individually with participants who you feel may be on the edge of their psychological safety zones.
- If a difficult situation arises, attempt to bring the participants who have a psychological problem back to the real world at their sensory/physical level (talk to them, touch them gently, describe the surroundings to them), mental level (remind them of day/hour, of where they are, and so on), and emotional level (tell them that they are fine, that you are staying with them and that everything is all right). It is usually a good idea to send the rest of the group away.
- Use other guidelines and techniques recommended by your organisation.

ENVIRONMENTAL SAFETY

Especially in the case of outdoor-based simulation games, you are likely to enter an outside physical and social environment and it is important to have this environment in mind during the game preparation and running. The basic considerations for running these games can be summarised as follows:

- Protected areas/preserves: Make sure you know the limits of these zones. If participants need to go through these zones, make it absolutely clear what areas are OK to enter and what are not. Remember that participants will be so involved in the game that they may forget about limits, so the best thing may be to give them a map with clearly marked areas.
- Private property: The great-looking field that you really need for running your game probably belongs to someone. It is imperative to check with the owners. There is nothing as bad as an angry farmer coming at you with his hungry dog during the peak of a game that just happened to ruin his year's crop.
- Social environment: If you run your games often in a particular area, the locals are probably used to seeing people on skis in the forest in the middle of the summer, pushing tyres on country roads or running around painted in colours. However, for most people these things are hard to comprehend without the full context and may result in some misunderstanding or bad feeling between you and them – potentially affecting your whole programme. The best thing you can do is to talk to the closest neighbours or mayor of the village before running the course or game.

PHYSICAL SAFETY

Obviously, you will follow the safety recommendations of your organisation, which vary from place to place and we will not elaborate on them here. On a more specific level, there are several important issues to prevent you from having problems with physical safety:

- Check the environment before the game: For outdoor games, you need to go to the terrain to see exactly what participants will encounter. You may have to go there several times and even run a simulation (run the game according to the key rules, as if you were a participant).

- First aid kits: Make sure the kits are accessible to participants – either the instructors should have them, or they should be given to participant groups in case they are acting away from the instructor's immediate access.
- Evacuation briefing: Staff need to know evacuation routes. If the participants are acting independently, you have to give them this information (perhaps in a sealed envelope which will include maps and key phone numbers).

PSYCHOLOGICAL AND EMOTIONAL SAFETY

There are many ways to prevent risks to participants' psychological well-being, but because of the nature of the instructor/participant interaction, the instructor's safety should also be considered. The best way to avoid psychological harm is to incorporate risk management into every stage of the preparation and running of the game. For example:

Staff
- Have at least one person in the team of instructors trained in a psychological discipline or working in a caring profession.
- It may help to facilitate the review in pairs; one person can observe the group while the other concentrates on the discussion.
- Give the team of instructors enough time off.
- Do not let any instructor run an activity if it could have a personal negative outcome.

Participants
- Try and predict problems which may result from your participant group when planning the games.
- Participants will open up emotionally more during the games than they usually do in their real lives and the new emotions may be very powerful for them, possibly resulting in unexpected behaviours. Be ready to lessen the intensity of any activity at any time and/or to intervene for specific participants.
- Sometimes, even a highly positive experience may result in temporary negative effects on the participant. For example, being able to feel whole may mean gaining access to previously hidden negative emotions, which may result in an immediate emotional shock as well as in a delayed shock reaction. Or a perceived ability 'to see things clearly now' may mean a personal crisis resulting in redefinition of a current personal situation or life plan for the participant. Therefore, watch even for the participants who demonstrate highly positive emotions – and not just during the particular game, but later on as well.
- Do not deprive participants of their resources – sleep, food, warmth, physical energy and also sense of time (removing watches is essentially a manipulative technique unless used sensitively).
- Be sensitive when you work with culturally mixed groups. A game that is perfectly tolerable by one culture may present a major emotional challenge from people from another culture.
- Make sure the participants always understand that the activity is voluntary or 'challenge by choice', but also make sure the peer pressure is not effectively cancelling this rule.
- Some participants may not be in full control of their emotions and cannot make a fully informed decision about participating in a particular activity. Be ready to recommend to them not to participate even if they say they are OK.

- Be careful of placing specific participants into situations with which they may have an emotional problem (for example, bringing a participant with claustrophobia into a cave or letting a person whose grandmother died recently play a grandmother during a role-play game).
- Be careful not to push participants to open up, even if you feel something is boiling under the surface. The participants have usually good reasons, even unconscious, to keep some problems private or unexplored.
- Some games incorporate an element of physical touch between men and women. Be aware of the fact that some of your participants may be love- or touch-deprived and will react to being touched (or to touching others) in an unusually powerful way.
- Some of the romantic relationships participants create on the course can be too powerful – they may be consuming the whole personalities of involved people and may affect the rest of the group as well. Make sure you do not enhance the intensity of the romantic relationship by your programme if such a situation happens. Think of ways to bring it to the ground gently.
- Some participants may use mental transferences to form a pseudo-romantic relationship towards an instructor, especially due to the perceived authority role of the instructor (that is, the participants may see the instructors not as who they are, but as their mothers, fathers, idols, and so on). The emotions generated by virtual transference may be fiercely positive and real, but very inappropriate. Do not get trapped and do not support the participants in building up their transference illusions.

Game considerations

- Do not present psychologically oriented games one after another.
- Make sure the psychologically oriented games are followed by enough time off and a good review.
- If you plan to run a psychologically intense game for the first time, the best thing is to simulate it with the team of instructors. If you are running an existing psychologically intense game that you personally have not run before, make sure you research it with people who have done it before or that you have an instructor in the game who knows the game.
- Do not run emotionally intense games less than three days before the end of the course.

In general, games incorporating some of the following elements may bring out strong emotions. If you present the elements in an appropriate context, these emotions will have a positive effect on participants – and vice versa:

- theme of death
- theme of romantic relationships
- physical exhaustion
- night activities
- meditations, guided visualisations and even physical relaxation
- face-painting/masks activities
- activities involving loud/trance/hard music or drumming
- many dancing activities
- some feedback activities
- some role-playing activities (allowing participants to express emotions they may be repressing).

3 *Games: Description and Logistics*

Daniela Zounková

8 *Games Introduction*

It's difficult to say which activities I learnt the most from as they were very well put together to fulfil the whole course... also the time between which had its own charm as well.
International course participant

Chapter overview

This chapter provides an introduction to the description and logistics for 30 games. The following four chapters split the games with emphasis on social, physical, creative or psychological activities. These are presented in alphabetical order in each chapter. The games are a selection, by the book authors and several senior instructors, of the most popular, frequently used and representative VSL games.

In presenting the methods and ideas for this book the authors have considered the element of risk involved in sharing these games and activities. The results of these concerns are presented in this disclaimer:

If you choose to use the activities and games you are responsible for assessing the suitability of any exercise for each individual within the group; from the point of view of their physical state of health and also their state of mind. In addition, you must make sure that each exercise is safe, and take whatever steps are appropriate in terms of people, materials or venue to ensure the safety of their participants. The authors assume no responsibility or liability for the use of the information presented in this book. This includes errors due to misprinting or omission of detail.

Game template

The template for each game is as follows:

1 Name of the game
2 Author
   Most of the games we present here have an author or team of authors. The games have
   often taken considerable time and effort to create and we reflect this by giving full credit
   to these authors. However, many – if not all – games are run in many modifications, each
   created by countless other anonymous authors.
3 Emphasis of the game (Figure 8.1)
   The emphasis of the games is split into the four main categories outlined throughout the
   book:
   – social games involving teams and/or strategy
   – physical games
   – creative games
   – psychological games with emotional emphasis aimed at self-reflection.

   The emphasis of the game is very subjective and depends greatly on the way you present
   the game, the time of day, how much time you give for the game, what is the motivation
   and debrief of the game. Use the emphasis as a guide and be ready to it to whatever your
   needs on the course are going to be. This flexibility relates even to the main emphasis of
   the game – you can be surprised that quite a few of the games can be framed and set up in
   a way that shifts their emphasis greatly.

   For example, the *Dance Hall* activity we present as a 'social game'; but it can fit under
   the 'physical game' heading if you put the emphasis on intense periods of dancing in a
   hot room. It can also be a 'reflective game', if you emphasise the aspect of going through
   various historical stages of the activity in a particular role and being exposed to all the
   good and bad that each stage brings; or it can be a 'creative game', if you let the
   participants create the historical events themselves, their roles and costumes, and so on.

4 Preparation time
5 Instructors for preparation
   The preparation time is based on an assumption that the game is being prepared by staff
   who are moderately experienced with the game. If you run the game for the first time,
   you will want to add about 20–30 per cent more time to the preparation. Note that the
   preparation of certain games may start a few days before the game runs and this time is
   not included in the overall preparation time. The preparation time does not include time
   related to the instructor's homework, i.e. thinking of the way to set up motivation,
   preparing the various props, setting the atmosphere for the game before the course,
   reading a book related to the game, or seeing a movie on which the game was based in
   order to be more aware of the origins of the game.
6 Materials needed
   Take this list as our suggestion only, as you might find creative ways to substitute for
   some materials or, on the contrary, bring in many more props to the game to make it
   more spicy.
7 Duration of the activity
   The game description is based on this duration of the game. Note that making the game

Scale: Low (L), Medium (M), High (H)

	Social	Physical	Creative	Reflective
Social games				
1 Auntie Amalda	H	L	M	M
2 Czech Dream Book	H	M	M	M
3 Dance Hall	H	M	M	M
4 Ecosystems	H	H	L	M
5 In the Skin of John Malkovich	H	L	M	H
6 Las Vegas	H	L	M	M
7 Poseidon	H	M	M	M
8 Running Letters	H	M	L	M
9 War of the Roses	H	L	M	M
Physical games				
1 Arena	M	H	L	L
2 Camel Trophy	H	H	L	M
3 Finnish Trail	M	H	L	L
4 Mountain Golf	M	H	L	L
5 Princess Shin-Sho	H	H	L	M
6 Sitting Game	M	H	L	L
Creative games				
1 Colour Mass	M	L	H	M
2 Dead Poets Society	L	L	H	H
3 Improvised Drama	M	M	H	M
4 Land Art	L	L	H	M
5 Pointillism	H	M	H	M
6 Rehearsal of the Orchestra	H	L	H	L
7 Wag the Dog	M	L	H	M
8 Web Pages	M	L	H	M
Psychological (reflective/emotional) games				
1 Games without Borders	M	L	M	H
2 Labyrinth of the World	M	L	M	H
3 Mars Venus	M	L	L	H
4 Nexus VI	H	H	L	H
5 Night Images	M	L	M	H
6 Stalker	M	H	L	H
7 Triffids	H	M	L	H

Figure 8.1   Emphasis of each game

shorter or longer might mean shifts in game emphasis, preparation time and overall outcome.

8 Number of instructors for activity
This number tells you how many instructors run the game. It can be lower, but we suggest that you work in lower numbers than suggested only after you get some experience with the game.

9 Number of participants
   The number of participants is just our estimate of what works best. In most cases, the game still should be effective if you adapt the rules to accommodate a different number of participants.

10 Location
   The suggested location is what has been proven to work best for this game. In the case of several games, the environment cannot be changed for another one (for example, it is hard to imagine to running *Camel Trophy* indoors).

11 Time of day
   As we suggested earlier in the text, changing the time is one of the greatest changing factors for the game. Any game can be run at any time – but with dramatically different outcomes. The description of the game fits the time of the day we suggest. Running the game at other times might change several of the parameters.

12 Game overview
   In the short overview, we present you with the main focus of the game and tell you very briefly what it entails.

13 Setting
   Relating to the location, we suggest what are some of the ideal parameters for the game environment.

14 Logistics
   This section describes the technical overview of the game, basic rules, instructor roles, and so on. For most of the games, this section is the core part to read. Please read it with an open mind – we cannot list all the situations that might happen during the games and mention only the main ones. Always plan for the unplanned, particularly in terms of risk management, and be ready to expand the game logistics to fit your course, instructors and participants.

15 Instructor hints
   If the logistics are the core of the game description, then the instructor hints are its shell. They help you run the game smoothly and list some of the common pitfalls or issues that might arise in the game or afterwards. Often, they come from the hands-on experience of instructors who have run the game before. So we present them here so that you do not have to reinvent the wheel and make the mistakes we made initially.

16 Introduction/motivation
   An area for your creativity! One game can be motivated or framed in a myriad of ways. We present here the most common motivation of the game. You might take it literally and repeat it the same way, or enhance it by using your own cultural elements or bits and pieces that fit your course. This part of the game is perhaps the most flexible one. It may help your understanding of some of the games to read the introduction/motivation sections first.

17 Possible modifications
   Any game can be modified and we list some of the changes we have incorporated – feel free to create your own!

9 *Social Games*

*I am feeling very privileged and blessed to
have had this time… to look at myself and
observe others being gently, sensitively
exposed to a myriad of challenges and
experiences that evoked so very much in
me.*
International course participant.

Chapter overview

The following games are presented in this chapter:

1 Auntie Amalda
2 Czech Dream Book
3 Dance Hall
4 Ecosystems
5 In the Skin of John Malkovich
6 Las Vegas
7 Poseidon
8 Running Letters
9 War of the Roses

1 Auntie Amalda

Author:	Světlana Horáková, Dalibor Naar
Social emphasis:	H
Physical emphasis:	L
Creative emphasis:	M
Psychological emphasis:	M
Preparation time:	1 hour
Instructors for preparation:	2–3
Material needed:	costumes, sound system and music, invitation letters for participants, last Will of Auntie, a cheque, family tree, and material to decorate the room
Duration of the activity:	2–3 hours (including dinner)
Number of instructors for activity:	4
Number of participants:	15–30
Location:	indoors
Time of the day:	evening

GAME OVERVIEW

A staged, little-structured game. A big family reunion changes dramatically into a hard negotiation over a large sum of money. Includes negotiation, communication training, team co-operation, creativity in role-play, relaxation and fun.

SETTING

Indoors, in a nicely decorated room reminiscent of an old manor house. Tables are prepared for a festive dinner. If there is the chance of taking participants to a special place where they have never been before (rent out a hall, perhaps), it helps the atmosphere.

INTRODUCTION/MOTIVATION

Auntie Amalda has inherited a large amount of money from her late husband. Now she is celebrating her birthday and has invited her wider family and elderly relatives. Her idea is to finalise her last Will, to decide who will get her £9 million pounds and with what results. So far, however, her relatives are oblivious to this fact. On her birthday all invited guests surround their auntie with friendliness and present the strangest gifts. They are also happy to meet one another after a long time, especially those who are closely related; all act in a rather friendly or politely reserved manner. At the start of a fantastic buffet, Auntie Amalda tells her guests that she would like to use this evening to decide on how to distribute her wealth. The person with the best solution ideas on spending the money will inherit all – a cheque for over £9 million! If she cannot decide, her last Will becomes effective by 10 p.m. However, before her guests have a chance to express their ideas (or right afterwards), Auntie Amalda dies while dancing a solo.

LOGISTICS

A well-dressed butler hands out envelopes containing personal invitations to the players during breaks between earlier activities, well before the evening. On the envelope or on the enclosed letter are the participant's new name and their relationship to Auntie Amalda. At the same time a family tree is published somewhere including the individual roles; everyone has time to find out with whom and how they are related. They have some time to prepare small gifts for their auntie and also to prepare a festive toast, celebration poem, dance, and so on. When the evening begins, participants (in costumes, playing the assigned roles) are welcomed by Auntie Amalda, hand over their gifts, and are led into the hall by the servants (instructors). They mingle and make polite conversation. Auntie Amalda then presents her faithful butler Jean (the instructor who leads the whole game), who is in charge of this evening. He is her right-hand man. She asks all to join her for dinner (which can be in another room). Before offering a toast, she explains why they have all been invited. 'Details will follow after dinner.' Dinner is a mixture of laughter, entertainment, participants elaborating their roles, plotting with other family members, and so on.

After dinner Auntie Amalda invites them to join in the dancing but first explains the conditions for acquiring her £9 million and then asks Jean to read out her last Will. If anyone has any thoughts on how they could or should inherit, she asks that they tell everyone present their particular ideas. During a dance solo – a full hour before the end of the time limit – Auntie Amalda suddenly and painfully suffers a heart attack and dies on the dance floor. Now the important part of the evening comes – participants (still in their roles) need to decide how they want to spend the £9 million. They all have to agree on one single purpose. If they do not, then according to Auntie Amalda's last Will, all the money will go on dogs' sweaters. Jean has the cheque and continually reminds everyone of the time left before 10 p.m. If participants unanimously agree on one idea, which is actually what is meant to happen, they can celebrate their decision. If not, it can be an interesting start to the review.

THE TEXT OF THE LAST WILL AND TESTAMENT OF AMALDA, COUNTESS OF AVONDALE
I, Amalda, Countess of Avondale, in full health of body and mind, do hereby bequeath my estate – the legacy of my late husband, the Count of Avondale – as follows:

- *To each of my dear relatives, who showed their love and affection by travelling such a long way to celebrate with me my birthday and our family reunion: £100 each.*
- *The full remaining sum – almost £9 million – I leave to the orphanage for lost animals in our little old village to be used for dog sweaters in cold winters. This last Will and Testament is to become effective today* [insert appropriate date] *at 10 p.m. However until that time, any member of my family will be invited to make any kind of proposal for an alternative use of the money. I will be willing and glad to support any good idea so the money can stay in the family.*

Amalda, Countess of Avondale
Signed on [insert the appropriate date] *in presence of Dr Graeme Nutshell*

INSTRUCTOR HINTS

- This game is built on the dramatic performances of the instructors playing Auntie and the Butler. Their appearance at the beginning of the game sets the tone for the whole evening. They should be good actors and agree beforehand on how exactly the evening is going to proceed.
- The main organisational person must be the Butler, as Auntie dies halfway through the game.
- If possible, include the dinner in the game. Make it as festive as possible; other instructors can play the roles of servants who attend at the tables.
- The branches of the family tree should be reasonably equal in size. The participants should receive a short description of their characters, their interests etc., so they can develop the roles, but still have scope to use their own creativity in expanding their character.

POSSIBLE MODIFICATIONS

The Auntie story can easily be replaced – the necessary part is the sudden break in the middle of the game where participants start to negotiate.

2 Czech Dream Book

Author:	Allan Gintel
Social emphasis:	H
Physical emphasis:	M
Creative emphasis:	M
Psychological emphasis:	M
Preparation time:	none
Instructors for preparation:	none
Material needed:	maps of the area
Duration of the activity:	8 hours to 3 days
Number of instructors for activity:	1
Number of participants:	8–100
Location:	outdoors
Time of the day:	daytime

GAME OVERVIEW

A specifically Czech game involving the spirit of *turistika* activities: enterprise, courage, communicative skills, meeting local people, learning about traditions and characteristic ways of living, and so on. Groups of participants wander through the countryside fulfilling given tasks and learning about the local environment.

SETTING

This activity requires inhabited countryside, preferably with small villages or settlements. Local people tend to be friendlier than in bigger towns, and there are probably more chances to help out with some tasks in the fields.

LOGISTICS

Participants are divided into groups of 2–5. They receive a list of tasks and a place where the whole group will meet again. They have to cover the distance between the starting point and the meeting point and to fulfil certain tasks along the way. The length of the journey and the nature of the tasks may vary depending on the goals of the game.

Possible tasks for one day could be:

- to find an interesting person and interview them
- to exchange a needle for an object, and then exchange this object at least five times and bring back something really special
- to help somebody and get invited to lunch
- to visit an interesting site (for example, a castle or chateau), find out about its history and write a legend about the place.

Possible tasks for two days or longer:

- to get free accommodation for one night offering your labour or services in exchange
- to visit a specific number of sites of historical interest from a given list
- to do some service work
- to rehearse a short theatrical performance and perform it in public – in a square of a little town, in a children's camp, and so on.

INSTRUCTOR HINTS

- This activity is very dependent on the context and habits of individual countries and cultures. However, be creative and try it out, as it usually results in a very exciting and fun expedition. People often accept when approached with offers to help out with work and like to talk to friendly visitors.
- It is useful to limit the amount of gear participants take with them. For a two-day journey, it is possible to send them out without sleeping bags when their task is to acquire accommodation from the locals. Travelling light makes participants try to communicate with the locals, and it also enables them to walk faster. However, in reality they are likely to spend a lot of time negotiating for a free overnight stay so although sleeping gear will make their backpacks heavier, their hearts will be lighter as they can enjoy the countryside and not worry too much about the night!
- Allowing a certain amount of money and some use of public transport allows greater freedom in choosing the journey and also makes it possible for the groups to cover greater distances (up to 250 km in 2.5 days). Give each group emergency envelopes with phone numbers and a certain amount of money, which can pay for the fares (train, bus) in case they are not able to make the meeting point on time.
- There must be basic rules given to all the groups, for example concerning hitchhiking or dividing the group.
- The size and way of putting the groups together offers many options. Smaller groups decide faster and it is easier for them to approach people. Bigger groups are safer for younger people, but decision making may be more difficult and some members may hide behind the others and not interact with the locals. Putting together people who like each other will make it a more pleasant experience, whereas choosing opposites will turn it into more of a communication and negotiation exercise.

• Make sure that your participants are versed in reading a map, the local train and bus schedules, and that they are able to communicate with the locals (that is, at least one person can speak the language).

POSSIBLE MODIFICATIONS

Think about the resources you have (the countryside, the locals, points of interest), your participants (young, old, locals, foreigners) and the goals you want to achieve (experience different cultures, practise decision making, learn to survive in a strange environment, and so on).

3 Dance Hall

Author:	Milena Holcová
Social emphasis:	H
Physical emphasis:	M
Creative emphasis:	M
Psychological emphasis:	M
Preparation time:	2.5 hours
Instructors for preparation:	2
Material needed:	props and costumes to characterise historic events, corresponding music, boom box, drinks and glasses for a bar, big mirror, spotlight, broom, names of decades written on large pieces of paper, roles summarised on small cards
Duration of the activity:	2–3 hours (+ extra hour for participants to prepare)
Number of instructors for activity:	1–2 for introduction, 1 for barman, (4–6 total)
Number of participants:	15–30
Location:	indoors and outdoors
Time of the day:	evening

GAME OVERVIEW

Little-structured drama-based game. Non-verbal expression of a specific character, focus on and empathy for the character, experiencing history, non-verbal communication, coping with changes. The game is based on the film *Dance Hall* (1950). Participants (playing roles) experience important moments of modern history in the setting of a dance hall.

SETTING

The room is arranged as a popular dance hall with a bar in one of the corners. By the entrance there is a big mirror hanging on the wall. The main motto is 'Time changes, characters stay the same.'

LOGISTICS

About one hour before the opening of the dance hall the instructors gather participants together. They are assigned characters, which have been carefully chosen by the team so they fit or maybe challenge participants. The descriptions of the characters must be simple, unambiguous and strong! Stress that it is supposed to be a performance. Those who play negative characters should not feel offended; it is usually easier to play negative roles. Participants receive information about which historical periods will be covered. It is necessary to stress that nobody speaks a word during the game! Characters can only express themselves with the help of gestures and actions. There is then a one-hour break for participants to think about their roles and prepare costumes and props.

At the given time the barman opens the dance hall. There is a big poster announcing the decade, and period music playing. The characters enter the room one after another. Each person stops in front of the big mirror and straightens their costume for the last time. This is also the moment to start acting their character. Once all the people are in the hall, they can start dancing, drink at the bar, pair off, and play their roles in any way they want. After a while, instructors (in costume) enter the dance hall and act out a sketch (for example, provoking a conflict), enabling all characters to take part. Once the events in the dance hall lose momentum, the barman stops the music and starts sweeping the floor. It is time to leave the dance hall (five-minute break) and change costumes for another era. After the break another historical period starts with different music and a new round begins. After the last historical period (modern day), the barman closes the bar, starts to put the chairs on the tables, and all the figures one after another leave the dance hall, glancing for the last time into the mirror. The game is over.

Examples of possible role descriptions:

- young romantic student coming from the country to the big city
- coward, nervous wreck, submissive type, needs to find a strong personality
- older, worldly-wise student
- dandy, overly self-confident, not too intelligent
- swindler and loafer who always knows how to acquire big money
- sensitive, emotional character, unstable, looking for constant support
- sincere and trusting person, pure in their ideals
- older teacher, proud of their country
- ascetic, serious type, reclusive, with strong inner drive
- soldier by profession, patriot and prototype of a hero
- feminist, ostentatiously independent
- cunning old actor tired by his life
- little unimportant white-collar worker, trying to please the boss
- anarchist, fighting the system – any system really
- trafficker, trying to make money from everybody and everything
- older man/woman, forsaken by their spouse, trying to find some excitement
- brave journalist who always stands on the battlefront
- good-humoured countryman/woman with common sense.

INSTRUCTOR HINTS

- The characterisations given here serve only as a guide. Instructors must think of characters that fit/challenge their own participants.
- Write all the character descriptions next to the real names of the participants on a big sheet of paper and place it in the dance hall so everybody can see it.
- The first period is short (10–15 minutes), the 1960s longer (20–30 minutes) and the end period can be longer (20+ minutes). The length of these episodes, and the game itself, depends on the ongoing atmosphere. It is up to the barman to judge this and direct the game accordingly. He should have at least 30 minutes of available music for each period.
- This game is extremely culture-dependent. Warning – the history of the past century can differ significantly, depending on what part of the world your participants come from (for example, Germany, Japan, Russia, and so on).
- Some historical events may not be universally known. Choose those which will be clearly understood by all.

INTRODUCTION/MOTIVATION

We are in a room that has for over one generation served as a popular dance hall. During the last seventy years, it has gone through the great depression, the war, liberation, after-war boom and euphoria, rock'n'roll, hippies and student strikes. Nowadays there is a disco, aerobics or break dancing. Historical periods, and eras, come and go. There are different people coming to the dance hall, one generation after another, the costumes and props change. What does not change are the types, the characters. Each generation has its cowards and heroes, strong and weak, stars and simpletons...

POSSIBLE MODIFICATIONS

- Modifications concern the historical content of the game. If you have a group all from the same country, use the most important events from their history (usually the past 100 years are included in the historical outline).
- It is possible to modify the whole historical aim of the game. For example, historical events can be replaced by music development (for example, 1920s music, Charleston, swing, jazz, Elvis Presley, rock'n'roll, Beatles, Abba, modern world).
- Participants can choose their own roles.

4 Ecosystems

Author:	Světlana Horáková
Social emphasis:	H
Physical emphasis:	H
Creative emphasis:	L
Psychological emphasis:	M
Preparation time:	1 hour
Instructors for preparation:	1
Material needed:	plan of the area, 'animals' (little pieces of fabric, plastic, wood, etc. in different colours), counting charts for referees, sheet with rules, charts for participants, pens, paper possibly a sound system with dynamic music
Duration of the activity:	2–2.5 hours
Number of instructors for activity:	1 + 1 for each team
Number of participants:	10–60
Location:	outdoors
Time of the day:	daytime

GAME OVERVIEW

A strategic team competition about preserving an ecosystem, which involves decision making and physical fitness (see 'rules for participants' for more specific aims).

SETTING

Outdoor setting, which is normally in a wood/forest. A plan is made of the local area the 'animals' of the ecosystems are placed at various sites up to 200 m away from the central control area.

LOGISTICS

Participants are divided into groups of 5–8. They are given written rules of the game (see 'rules for participants' for more specific details) and have some time to study them. After that, there is time to answer questions and elaborate on the rules. For example, how many people (1–2) need to stay in the base each 'year', keep the statistics and manage the running members of the team, and so on – these members must be changed after each year.

INSTRUCTOR HINTS

- Each instructor needs to understand the rules and know how to use the score charts before the game starts (see Figure 9.1).
- A plan of the area should be given to participants indicating the sites where the various animals are placed (usually about 100–200 m from the base).
- Approximately 50–100 of each animal are needed. These can be creatively printed on laminated paper or made from different coloured beads/models.
- Experienced instructors can keep scores for two teams at the same time – but only after they have thoroughly learned how to use the charts.
- It is a good idea to have one instructor responsible for announcing the time intervals – as the participants continually come and go. It is also a good motivation factor. It is possible to make special tape recordings with spring, summer, autumn or winter music, each of which lasts for exactly five minutes. In this way, participants can tell, according to the music, what season they are in.
- During the breaks, it is good to check whether there are enough animals in all of the sites. Their results have been counted so the animals can be used again.
- The results can be revealed during the review. From the chart, it is possible to count the efficiency of each team (from the overall number of runs and the final number of points gained), its development during the years, and the number of 'dead' animals (that is, those which were brought but were not fed).
- Participants should drink enough water during the running part.

POSSIBLE MODIFICATIONS

If there is not enough time, the time intervals can be shortened (the season lasts only four minutes) and the sites could be closer.

RULES FOR PARTICIPANTS

Each team is a provider (supplier) for three ecosystems. These ecosystems function absolutely independently. Each of them has a certain food chain – one organism is food for the next one (a frog eats a mosquito; a stork eats the frog). Each animal must have enough food to survive. In this case 'enough' means twice as many (for example, in order to survive one year, 1 shark needs 2 snappers, one snapper needs 2 herrings and 1 herring needs 2 seaweeds; so 8 seaweeds are needed to support 1 shark). This feed-to-survive ratio is the same in all the ecosystems. The list of the ecosystems including the feed-to-survive ratio is as follows:

SHARK	SNAPPER	HERRING	SEAWEED
1	2	4	8

STORK	FROG	MOSQUITO
1	2	4

STOAT	SQUIRREL	NUT
1	2	4

The aim of the game is to get the greatest number of sharks, storks and stoats – the animals highest in the food chain. You must get at least one of each of these. The following points are allocated to the animals: SHARK – 4, STORK – 3, STOAT – 3. The final result of the game depends on the total number of points in total. Each team will participate in three years of the life of the ecosystems. Each year runs for 20 minutes, and is divided into four different seasons – each five minutes long. During this time, the animals (food) can be collected from the particular sites (these are placed at various distances around the base). The Ecosystems season plan is given to participants and illustrates the multiplication factor for each animal during each season (see Figure 9.2). The seasons change continually and this is always announced loudly. Each year is followed by a 10-minute break.

One person may visit one site at a time and collect only one animal during each run from the base. The animal collected from the site will be multiplied (reproduced) according to the season in which it was collected and announced. The multiplication ratio is stated in the tables. If the ratio is zero, the organism does not have its living conditions fulfilled and it dies when it is collected. The multiplication will occur only at the moment when the animal is collected – once in the whole game. To feed an animal means to have food for it at the end of the year in which it was collected. At this time, there is an annual tally taken and the points are given for the highest animals that have been fed. The animals that did not have enough food to survive (at any level of the ecosystem) are eliminated from the game (they 'die'). Other unused animals are transferred to the next year.

If a stork was fed (given two frogs and the two frogs were given four mosquitoes in the same year), the team gets three points for the stork and all animals that have been eaten are eliminated from the game. The stork (the highest animal evaluated by points) is not to be looked after anymore. Each collected animal has to be immediately announced to the assigned instructor. The instructor will write down the season when it was collected and the animal will automatically be calculated by the appropriate multiplying ratio. The instructor's records cannot be consulted during the game and the team needs to keep its own tally. The previous year is analysed during the 10-minute break and the team can prepare its strategy for the next year based on the results. Once the break has started, you are not allowed to leave base. If an animal is collected during the break, it can be announced in the following year. The animals that have been collected from the sites cannot be stored before declaring them.

Team:	Year	Spring	Σ	Summer	Σ	Autumn	Σ	Winter	Σ	Σ	Survive	Eaten	Left
Seaweed		×4		×6		×3		×3					
Herring		×4		×6		×4		×4					
Snapper		×1		×2		×2		×1					
Sharks		×3		×2		×1		×1					

Σ Sharks: Points:

Mosquito		×4		×5		×2		×0					
Frogs		×2		×2		×2		×1					
Storks		×3		×1		×0		×0					

Σ Storks: Points:

Nuts		×0		×2		×4		×3					
Squirrels		×2		×2		×1		×0.5					
Stoats		×2		×2		×1		×1					

Σ Stoats: Points:

Points from the last year: Points for this year: Points in total:

Figure 9.1 Ecosystems score sheet

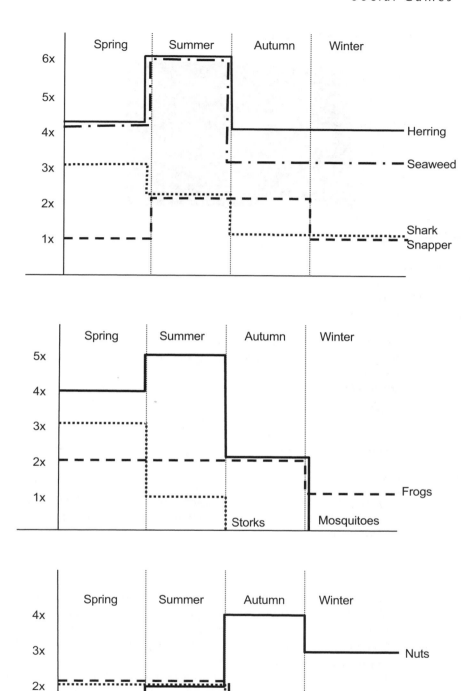

Figure 9.2   Ecosystems season plan

5 In the Skin of John Malkovich

Author:	Dan Franc
Social emphasis:	H
Physical emphasis:	L
Creative emphasis:	M
Psychological emphasis:	H
Preparation time:	2 hours
Instructors for preparation:	1
Material needed:	'teleport' and equipment for simple initiative games
Duration of the activity:	4 hours
Number of instructors for activity:	1 + 1 for each group of participants
Number of participants:	8–30
Location:	indoors and outdoors
Time of the day:	daytime

GAME OVERVIEW

Psychological, role-play game based on the film *Being John Malkovich* (1999). Participants adopt the identity of somebody else and have a chance to see another person playing themselves, and receive feedback.

LOGISTICS

Two days before the game, participants write the names of five people on the course they know the best and three names of people they know the least. This information is then used for the assigning of new identities. One day before the game, posters appear offering a lifetime experience – an opportunity to see the world through the eyes of somebody else. Those who want to try need to sign up for the game.

After the introduction/motivation, an instructor in the role of John Malkovich explains the rules. Participants will receive a new identity after they go through the 'teleport' (any kind of pipe or darkened narrow space with two openings). Somebody else will receive their existing identity so they will get a chance to see themselves from the outside. During the length of the change, there will be the normal course programme running in which participants will take part, but in their new identities. The change lasts two to three hours. After that, they will become themselves again. Identities must be changed in such a way that everybody gets to play somebody they know rather well. Ideally, there will be groups of 6–10 participants, which include people who play each other.

Each participant prepares a set of clothes for the new person who will impersonate them. After the teleport, participants must wear their new clothes, a nametag with their new name, and everybody must call them by that name (including instructors), and behave as if they were that person. It is a good idea to include some name activities at the beginning so everybody gets a chance to get used to the new names. After that, groups take part in some easy activities (team dynamics exercises). There can (and should) be activities that participants have done earlier on the course so the role-play becomes more important than the solution of the task itself. After each activity, there is a short review of the process, but participants keep to their roles. Before they become themselves, there should be time for them to write a letter to the person they were impersonating – 'What was it like to be you?' The letter is sealed and handed to John Malkovich before each participant goes through the teleport in the opposite direction and becomes themselves again. Letters are delivered after participants are back in their real identities.

INSTRUCTOR HINTS

- The whole activity must be strictly optional – those who decide not to take part stay as themselves but they should still respect the new identities of the others and behave accordingly.
- The activity should be introduced only after participants have had a chance to get to know each other – otherwise they will not know the person they have to impersonate.
- Gender is not important – males can play females and vice versa. It is the character which is of interest. The same applies to the size of clothes. Everything can be adjusted. Be careful who you choose to play participants who have some visible handicap – stutter, limp, and so on. Choosing a weak actor for somebody like this may result in stressing just this one characteristic.
- It can be a good challenge for participants to play somebody who has a very different character from their own – dominant people in the group get to play someone shy who stays mostly in the background, and so on. For the shy participants, it can be a good opportunity to assert themselves in the group.
- The teleport must be prepared properly, especially the show around it so participants really get the feeling that it is a big thing. On the way back to their normal self, welcome them, repeat their names and guide them back to reality. For some it can be difficult to be outside of their body for some time.
- The activities included in this game should be quite structured, with clear rules, so the acting can take precedence. Rules that are too difficult can result in the participants concentrating on the game itself, rather than on their new roles. Easier dynamics work best.
- Topics for review: questions of identity; unpleasant feeling from somebody using my things, accepting the role of somebody else, responsibility for playing another person, somebody plays me incorrectly and gives a wrong message about me, meeting myself – how does it feel?

INTRODUCTION/MOTIVATION

John Malkovich is a former actor who found out that his body could work as a special type of portal. He can lend his body to other people who then see the world through his eyes and participate in his world – they become John Malkovich for a specified period of time. Malkovich made a profitable business out of this exchange and travelled around the globe offering people his special services. For motivation, it is advisable to change one instructor into another (wear a wig, shave, change clothes, and so on) so participants get the idea quickly.

POSSIBLE MODIFICATIONS

It is possible to make the game longer, and even play it overnight. The change of identities takes place late in the evening with participants spending the night in the bed of the person they are impersonating, having breakfast and staying in their roles for part of the morning programme.

6 Las Vegas

Author:	Vlád'a Halada
Social emphasis:	H
Physical emphasis:	L
Creative emphasis:	M
Psychological emphasis:	M
Preparation time:	2 hours
Instructors for preparation:	2
Material needed:	roulette wheel and table, tokens, signs for bar and bank, drinks and refreshment for the bar, costumes, decoration of the room, blank bills of exchange, reflectors, boom box, music for atmosphere
Duration of the activity:	2–3 hours
Number of instructors for activity:	4
Number of participants:	15–60
Location:	indoors
Time of the day:	evening, night

GAME OVERVIEW

Little-structured drama-based fun game for breaking down barriers and building bonds between participants. Social evening in a casino with gambling and an auction at the end.

SETTING

The room is arranged as a casino. There is one (or more) table with roulette, bar, bank (possibly some more gambling options, such as card games). Try to create a festive atmosphere, high society, costumes and music. Participants are welcomed with a toast.

LOGISTICS

After the introductory invitation to the Casino there is time for participants to prepare – find a costume, think of a role they want to play (young aristocrat, factory owner and his wife, vamp, pickpocket). The rules of the whole game, as well as for roulette, are explained after everybody has entered the casino. The money needed for participation in the game (roulette, cards, bar, and so on) can be obtained from the bank, by using a 'bill of exchange'. On each bill of exchange, participants write a tangible service, which they are able to offer and fulfil. This bill of exchange is valid for one year of real time, not just on the course, and this bill of exchange is offered to the bank, who evaluates the service and buys it for a certain amount of money. Participants can sell their bills of exchange during the game until just before the 'auction'. During the evening participants gain or lose money – at the roulette table, cards, bar, and so on. At the end of the evening, there is an auction and participants can buy other people's bills of exchange by bidding for them. The new owners of the bills can claim the services at any time during the following year. Examples of possible services to offer:

- to walk a dog
- to wash a car by hand
- to bake a cake and take it to the owner of the bill
- to sing a love song under the window
- to teach a certain skill
- to organise a skiing/biking/sightseeing trip for 1–2–x people for 1–2–x days
- to dance on the table right after the game is over
- to invite you to dinner/theatre/movies
- to prepare breakfast and bring it to your bedside
- to compose a celebration poem and recite it in front of all the people on the course
- to give a massage.

INSTRUCTOR HINTS

- Roulette is played according to usual rules of the game – participants bet a certain amount of money on a number, couple, triplet, dozen, even or odd numbers, black or red numbers. The sum is multiplied depending on the odds of the bet placed in the case of the spinning ball resulting in a winning bet.
- All money and tokens used in the casino are fake! They have nothing to do with real money and are only valid for the one night. At the end of the game, they lose their value.
- The roulette is played in rounds (approximately three rounds, each with 10 throws). During the breaks, the atmosphere can be animated with little competitions – arm-wrestling, dance competition, and so on. There should be some financial prize for the winners.
- Have a list of suggested services at the bank so participants can get some ideas about what they can actually sell. Of course, the more creative and funny the service is, the more money the participants get for it. The services, in general, should be of such a nature that they could not be bought for normal money.
- The service on the bill of exchange needs to be thoroughly specified; that is, what exactly is offered, how many times (or for how long), what other sub-services are included, and so on.
- All the instructors operating individual spots in the casino need to have agreed on the value of the money before the game, so that the prices in the bar correspond with the amounts of cash participants are able to get from the bank and/or lose at roulette.
- In certain cultures gambling may be seen as an inappropriate activity. Be aware of this and check before you decide to play this game!

INTRODUCTION/MOTIVATION

Instructors, dressed as staff (or owners) of the casino come in front of the participants during the preceding activity or dinner and invite them to a social evening in a casino, and everything that goes with it. They stress the proper attire, time and place of the meeting.

7 Poseidon

Author:	Milena Holcová
Social emphasis:	H
Physical emphasis:	M
Creative emphasis:	M
Psychological emphasis:	M
Preparation time:	2–3 hours
Instructors for preparation:	2–3
Material needed:	uniforms for instructors, material to decorate the room (paper lanterns, garlands, etc.), music/sounds (hooter, sound of rushing water), visual effects (stroboscope, beacon), ropes, rope ladders, water hose, water buckets, costumes for participants
Duration of the activity:	3 hours
Number of instructors for activity:	5–6
Number of participants:	15–30
Location:	indoors (Part 1), outdoors (Part 2)
Time of the day:	evening, night

GAME OVERVIEW

Dramatic role-play game, based on the 1960s disaster movie *The Poseidon Adventure*. Participants become passengers on the *Poseidon*. The cruise ship is on its way from the USA to Australia on New Year's Eve 1952. Just after midnight a huge wave, from an underwater nuclear experiment, hits the ship. The air chamber of the ship prevents it from sinking, but the wave turns it upside down. Those who survive the disaster have oxygen left for just a couple of hours. The only way to be saved is to find the way to the keel and chop through the bottom of the ship next to the propeller. Passengers are 'saved' by overcoming a number of demanding obstacles testing/challenging skilfulness, courage, strength and group co-operation. Features are surprise, team co-operation and problem solving under time pressure.

SETTING

Part 1: a beautifully decorated room for the New Year's Eve celebration (lanterns, candles, semi-darkness, card tables). Nobody should suspect that there is a disaster on the way! Toasts, nice music and a festive atmosphere.

Part 2: after the disaster participants start to make their way to the 'keel', which is a difficult track full of demanding obstacles (crawling under cars, climbing over walls or out of windows, through buildings, ruins of an old house, low rope obstacles, ladders, maze made of ropes, crawling through pipes and/or huge tyres, and so on).

LOGISTICS

Each participant plays the role given to them. When creating the characters, organise people into families; for example, married couples, their children, brothers and sisters, a family with servants, and so on. Participants wearing appropriate costumes come to the decorated room. They are divided into three travelling classes, following the tradition of ocean cruises: first, second and third class (see modifications section for hints on how to divide them). The captain of the ship introduces his crew (instructors). Dinner is served (different types of food for individual classes) and participants develop their roles. After dinner, there is entertainment and dancing. As midnight comes closer the excitement rises, then at midnight, champagne, toasts...

Just after midnight, disaster strikes. Total darkness, smoke, sounds of breaking china, hooter and hurtling water, screaming people, chaos. The captain tells everyone what has happened and asks them to follow him. According to the number of participants, it is possible to split the group into two, which go through the second part of the game separately. At each obstacle participants are given a short brief, and told what resources and time they have available. These participants who do not overcome the obstacle within the time limit, 'die'. Time pressure is important and in the hands of the group's instructor, manipulates the dynamics of the game (that is, when participants 'die'). The number and nature of the obstacles depends on the centre's surroundings. If feasible, get participants wet (crawling under a car, where a water hose is installed, through showers, stream, and so on) to make the simulation as real as possible.

What can be expected during the game? Panic, mob hysteria, euphoria, gradual division of roles within the group, natural leaders emerging. Parallel to the increasing difficulty of the obstacles and growing stress, participants start to put their roles aside, family ties disintegrate, and people start fighting for their lives (interesting review topic). The final obstacle should simulate meeting the surviving passengers and the rescue team (those that have died). At the end there is a celebratory hot drink.

INSTRUCTOR HINTS

- The game is logistically demanding. You need to have everything ready, even for the second part of the game, before it all starts.
- The instructor(s) leading the group(s) in Part 2 must have good timing. The group cannot lose all its strong members at the initial obstacles otherwise it will not be able to deal with

those that come later! There should be at least five people (in each group) 'alive' at the end of the journey.

- The obstacles should increase in difficulty as the game progresses.
- 'Dead' participants follow the group and observe, but are not allowed to speak or interfere in any way with those who are still 'alive'.
- At the end of the game, there should be hot drinks and blankets available. Finish close to the centre so participants can change their wet clothes immediately.
- The amount of water involved must be guided by the weather conditions. If it is too cold outside, do not let the participants run around in wet clothes for too long.
- Some obstacles may be difficult for people prone to different kinds of phobias (claustrophobia, fear of water, and so on). Find out before you introduce the game!

INTRODUCTION/MOTIVATION

The captain of the ship (with appropriate jacket and cap) formally invites participants to join the cruise. Examples of roles:

First class
- Peter Johnson (49), a rich businessman, self-made man
- Annie Johnson (43), his wife
- Mary-Anne Johnson (19), their daughter, artistic and romantic soul
- Peter Johnson Jr. (14), spoilt youngest son
- Sir Frederic Ashley (75), head of an old noble English family
- Victor Laconte (31), young millionaire, inherited all his fortune from his uncle
- Miss Andrea Bunuela (18), the only daughter of Argentina's Prime Minister
- Theodora García (56), her nanny, now her escort.

Second class
- Marcel Kowalski (60), university professor of botany
- John Greenspan (35), engineer, inventor
- Eve Greenspan (25), his wife
- Drita Skruhi (41), hairdresser
- Nadesan Narenthiran (50), Indian merchant
- Kiana Narenthiran (42), his wife, quite conservative
- Bhavin Narenthiran (21), their son, very pro-European views
- George White (63), army lieutenant, retired.

Third class
- Rado Kovacz (45), manual worker trying to find a job abroad
- Nora Kovacz (44), faithful wife, who has left three of her children at home
- Rita Kovacz (16), one of their daughters, has worked since she was a little child
- Elene Kovacz (70), Rita's grandmother; this is her first sea journey
- Martha Nightale (quite young), girl of bad repute
- Tanja Gregoriana (young), cheerful, independent girl
- Sean McHonningan (40), music-hall artist.

POSSIBLE MODIFICATIONS

There are many ways of classifying participants for the first part of the game. They can draw lots or choose roles from a list according to their taste. Another possibility is to use the results of some previous game – winners become the first class passengers, defeated team the third class, the rest stay in the second class.

8 Running Letters

Author:	Jiří Brožek, Michal Bauer, Jana Chaloupková
Social emphasis:	H
Physical emphasis:	M
Creative emphasis:	L
Psychological emphasis:	M
Preparation time:	1 hour
Instructors for preparation:	1
Material needed:	playing board, letters on the sites, pens, papers, sets of rules for each of the teams, running plan (see below), dictionary
Duration of the activity:	1.5–2 hours
Number of instructors for activity:	3
Number of participants:	10–30
Location:	outdoors
Time of the day:	daytime

GAME OVERVIEW

Strategic physical game, involving running for letters and then making words, seeking to promote creativity, team management and physical fitness.

SETTING

Natural environment, clear forest or a meadow. A map of the surroundings is made and individual sites with the letters are indicated (sites are approximately 100–200 m from the base).

LOGISTICS

Participants are divided into groups of four to seven. They are given written rules of the game (see 'rules for participants' for more specific details) and have some time to study them and ask questions, and then the game starts. Participants run to different sites to get the letters, and then try to make up words on the board and score maximum points. The roles of the individual members in the team are not strictly set – they can run for letters, or they can stay by the playing board and decide about the words. It is up to the team to organise themselves.

The number of letters in the game is limited. They are all indicated on the running plan (a list of letters as they are stored on the sites – see below). Participants can only use those letters which they have brought from the sites. Before they run to the site, they need to indicate on the running plan where they are going and what letter they are bringing. The instructor operating the running plan will cross that letter off so everybody knows it is no longer available. The instructor who operates the playing board places the letters on it, and participants need to stay back from it. This instructor also counts the number of points for each word placed on the board. If there are more teams wishing to place words on the board at the same time, they need to take turns.

INSTRUCTOR HINTS

- One instructor (who is good at maths) operates the playing board during the game; another one is needed for the running plan; the last should serve as the main umpire who solves any problems that may arise during the activity.
- It is a good idea to have a dictionary available, as there may be disagreements as to whether words are acceptable.
- The playing board can be produced in many different ways. If you plan to play the game only once, a large sheet of paper and markers are OK. If you plan to use it repeatedly, letters can be made of cardboard or any harder material with Velcro® on the reverse side. The playing board is then made from a piece of carpet so Velcro® can stick to it.

RULES FOR PARTICIPANTS

Rules for the team
1 Letters are available at the sites, as indicated on the map.
2 Each runner can only visit one site at a time and only bring one letter back.
3 Before running, each runner needs to announce to the person at the running plan which site they are going to and what letter they will bring back.
4 If any discrepancy arises, the runner is not allowed to take a different letter from the site. The referee will rule on the problem in a way that no team is discriminated against.

Rules for the players at the playing board
1 General
   The game consists of forming interlocking words, crossword fashion, on the Running Letters playing board (see Figure 9.3) using letters with various score values. Each team competes for the highest score by using their letters in combinations that take best advantage of letter values. The members of the team are continually bringing the letters.

List of letters and their score values

A1	F4	K8	P4	U1	Z8
B4	G2	L2	Q8	V4	Blank
C4	H4	M4	R2	W4	
D2	I1	N2	S2	X8	
E1	J8	O1	T2	Y4	

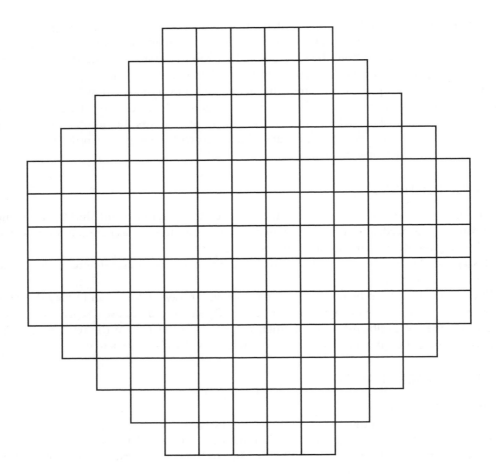

Figure 9.3   Running Letters playing board

2 The playing board
   A hexagonal grid consisting of 129 squares forms the playing board (see Figure 9.3).
3 The beginning of the game
   Any of the players at the playing board can make the first word by combining two or more letters (using the instructor operating the playing board). One of the letters must be placed at the centre square. There is no set order in which the players should lay down other new words.
4 Play
   – The first player combines two or more letters to form a word and places them on the board to read either across or down with one letter on the centre square. Diagonal words are not permitted.
   – Counting the points, which the referee records, completes the turn.
   – Other players (as the letters continually brought back by their teams allows them) add one or more letters to those already played so as to form new words. All letters played at any one turn must be put in one row across or down the board. They must form a complete word and if, at the same time, they touch other letters in adjacent rows, these

too must form complete words, crossword fashion, with all such letters. The player gets full credit for all words formed or modified (the scores of letters played before are also counted if they become a part of a new word or modification).
- New words can be formed by:
  - Adding one or more letter to a word or letters already on the board.
  - Placing a word at right angles to a word already on the board. The new word must use one of the letters already on the board or must add a letter to it (see Turns 2, 3, 4).
  - Placing a complete word parallel to a word already played so adjoining letters also form complete words (see Turn).
- No letter can be moved after it has been played.
- The two blank cards can be used as any letter desired. When playing a blank the player must state what letter it represents, after which it cannot be changed during the game.
- Any words found in a standard dictionary are permitted except those starting with capital letters, those designated as foreign words, abbreviations, or words requiring apostrophes or hyphens. Consult a dictionary to check spelling.
- In the case of any disputes, the referee at the playing board has the final decision.

5 The end of play
Play can be finished in two ways:
- When one of the teams lays down their entire stock of letters and no others are available for them to collect from the sites.
- The referee at the playing board ends play after the pre-announced time limit expires.

6 Scoring
- The referee at the playing board keeps a tally of each team's score. A number at the bottom of the card indicates the score value of each letter. The score value of a blank is zero.
- The score for each turn is the sum of the values of all of the letters in each word formed or modified in the play. Each team may double or triple their word score by playing once in the game a:
  - Double word card, which doubles the score of the entire word;
  - Triple word card, which triples the word score.
- The above word premiums apply only in the turn in which they are first played. In subsequent turns letters count at face value.
- When two or more words are formed in the same play, each is scored. The common letter is counted in the score for each word (see examples, Turn 3, 4 below).
- Any team that plays seven or more letters in a single turn automatically scores a premium of triple the word score (a double or triple word score card cannot be played in this case).
- At the end of the game each team's score is reduced by the sum of their un-played letters in hand. Un-played double or triple word cards count zero.

Examples of word formation and scoring

In the following, the words added in five successive plays are shown in heavy type. The scores shown are the correct scores if the letter R is placed on the centre square. In Turn 1 count **HORN**; in Turn 2 **FARM**; in Turn 3 **PASTE** and **FARMS**; in Turn 4, **MOB**, **NOT**, and **BE**; in Turn 5, **BIT**, **PI**, and **AT**.

Turn 1: Score 9   Turn 2: Score 11   Turn 3: Score 23

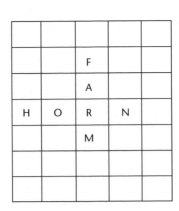

Turn 4: Score 19   Turn 5: Score 15

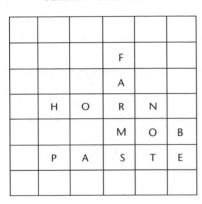

This is the list of letters (and their values) to be placed at the individual checkpoints (needs to be copied onto a large piece of paper which serves as the running plan):

1 A1, A1, D2, E1, E1, H4, I1, L2, N2, O1, R2, S2, T2, U1
2 A1, A1, D2, E1, F4, I1, I1, L2, N2, O1, R2, S2, T2, U1
3 A1, B4, D2, E1, F4, I1, I1, N2, O1, O1, R2, S2, T2, U1
4 A1, B4, E1, E1, G2, I1, L2, N2, O1, O1, R2, S2, T2, Y4
5 A1, C4, E1, E1, G2, I1, L2, N2, O1, P4, R2, T2, U1, Y4
6 A1, C4, E1, E1, G2, I1, K8, M4, N2, P4, R2, V4, W4, X8, BLANK
7 A1, D2, E1, E1, H4, I1, J8, M4, O1, Q8, T2, V4, W4, Z8, BLANK
8 A1, D2, E1, E1, H4, I1, L2, M4, O1, R2, S2, S2, V4, V4, U1, Y4, BLANK

Checkpoint number 8 is fictitious. When participants come to the checkpoint, they find a note 'Sorry, this checkpoint does not contain any letters.' It is up to them to spread the information among the other members of their team so others do not run there in vain.

9 War of the Roses

Author:	Antonín Rosický, Jiří Walder
Social emphasis:	H
Physical emphasis:	L
Creative emphasis:	M
Psychological emphasis:	M
Preparation time:	30 minutes
Instructors for preparation:	1
Material needed:	membership cards, large sheet of paper for announcing the revealed participants, distinctive music
Duration of the activity:	2–3 days
Number of instructors for activity:	1
Number of participants:	6–30
Location:	indoors and outdoors
Time of the day:	any time

GAME OVERVIEW

Communication game running in the background of a normal programme. Inspired by historical events in the English Wars of the Roses. Two families fulfil various tasks. None of the participants know at the beginning of the game to which family they belong.

LOGISTICS

Participants can decide not to take part, or they can play at any time. The game can run in parallel to other activities for several days. After the introduction each participant receives a membership card. Most of the cards are empty, but it is announced that several players have a letter on their cards: L = Lancaster, Y = York. From that moment on, both families carry out various tasks. The tasks are announced when all the participants are present (during lunch, for example). The main task is for individual family members to fulfil all the announced tasks. At the same time, each participant must try to gain as many new members as possible to strengthen their family's ranks. The tasks become more demanding and it is not possible to carry them out without a good working team. However, members of the individual families cannot be revealed. Therefore all the activities need to be carried out secretly, with great caution. A player becomes a member of a family when they write the letter L or Y on their membership card. After that, it is not possible to change the choice. If the players behave discretely, it is very difficult to learn to which family they belong (if any). To gain new members to their team, players need to persuade others (with unmarked cards) that their team is the one that will win.

If a player believes that they know a member of the competing family, they can come to the instructor and reveal them. This can only be done by a person who is already in the game (that is, has one of the letters on their card). The instructor then discretely asks the 'revealed person' to present their card. If they really are a member of the competing family, they are officially revealed. Their card is taken away from them, their name announced on a large sheet of paper and their participation in the game is over. However, if this participant is neutral in the game (no letter on their card), or even belongs to the same family, the card is taken away from the person who made the denouncement. All the revealed participants are out of the game and cannot participate any longer.

Examples of the tasks:

- tomorrow morning each of the teams need to have their flag (a big, representative one) hanging on the tree in front of the centre
- any helpful activities for the centre – cutting wood, cleaning, bringing rubbish from the forest, and so on
- to bring a stone, as big as possible, and place it in front of the centre
- to build a construction as tall as possible.

INSTRUCTOR HINTS

- Stress that it is not the aim of the game to destroy the other family's work. It is to establish contacts, to expand the family and to try to reveal the opponents. Any participant can inquire and/or disclose their membership to anybody. What goes on between individual participants, is entirely up to them; plotting is an integral part of the game.
- Distinctive music is played whenever something connected to the game happens.

INTRODUCTION/MOTIVATION

After the end of the Hundred Years' War with France, the English nobility return home and start fighting each other to take control. The country is divided into two competing families, the Yorks and the Lancasters, who fight against each other to gain the royal crown. This war was called 'The Wars of the Roses' because the Yorks had a white rose in their coat of arms, while the Lancasters had a red rose as their symbol. In the year 1455 Richard, the Duke of York, started an uprising, which gradually grew into a merciless war. The victory ranged from one side then to the other. Eventually, the Yorks won. Richard lost his life, but his son Edward became the King of England in 1461 after the battle of Towton.

10 *Physical Games*

*Overall a more holistic challenge, people
taken out of comfort zones physically,
spiritually, emotionally, creatively and
socially.*
International course participant

Chapter overview

The following games are presented in this chapter:

1 Arena
2 Camel Trophy
3 Finnish Trail
4 Mountain Golf
5 Princess Shin-Sho
6 Sitting Game.

1 Arena

Author:	Unknown
Social emphasis:	M
Physical emphasis:	H
Creative emphasis	L
Psychological emphasis:	L
Preparation time:	0.5 hour
Instructors for preparation:	2
Material needed:	ropes or paper streamers to mark the track, stopwatch
Duration of the activity:	1 hour
Number of instructors for activity:	2
Number of participants:	minimum 20
Location:	outdoors
Time of the day:	daytime

GAME OVERVIEW

Physical running team competition with simple rules. Physical challenge involving team co-operation.

SETTING

Activity held outdoors around a track approximately 150 m long with no obstacles. Racing stables lie on the inside of the track with openings approximately 1 m wide and clearly marked.

LOGISTICS

Participants are divided into groups of five to seven. Each team is placed in one of the stables. After the start, each team sends one pair racing around the track. They try to catch up with the pair running in front of them. For overtaking one pair, the team gets one point. There is also one point for finishing one round. During the whole circuit, the pair holds hands and they cannot split; if that happens, the team loses one point. After finishing one round, the pair can either run into the stable and another pair starts on the track immediately, or they can do another circuit. If, during the changeover, the stable is overtaken by another team there is also a point lost. The whole race has several rounds. The first round takes 10 minutes of continuous racing. After this round the results are announced. There is time to relax and to decide on strategy. In the next round, the racing goes in the other direction on the track. The teams are responsible for counting their points and the main referee is kept informed. The number of rounds in the whole competition depends on the age and physical condition of the participants, and also on the amount of time available.

INSTRUCTOR HINTS

- The number of participants in the teams does not necessarily have to be even – an uneven number means team members need to swap in the pairs.
- Each of the racing pairs should carry a scarf. When the next pair takes over, they need to take the scarf from the previous pair. When there are people standing around, the scarf makes it easier to recognise the actual couple being overtaken.
- The activity is physically demanding, so a thorough warm-up is needed. Watch participants who have a medical condition and have first aid kits present.
- There needs to be enough to drink during the whole game. Encourage the participants to take plenty of liquid.

2 Camel Trophy

Author:	Jan Bláha
Social emphasis:	H
Physical emphasis:	H
Creative emphasis:	L
Psychological emphasis:	M
Preparation time:	2–3 hours
Instructors for preparation:	3
Material needed:	big tractor tyres, ropes, harnesses, helmets, maps and orienteering lanterns
Duration of the activity:	2–5 hours
Number of instructors for activity:	4–5
Number of participants:	10–30
Location:	outdoors
Time of the day:	daytime

GAME OVERVIEW

Physical fitness, stretching personal limits, challenge, bonding in the group. Physically very demanding game, team competition where huge tyres represent off-road vehicles. Inspired by the off-road competition of the same name.

SETTING

Natural outdoor environment, preferably with water – small streams, lakes, and so on. Tyres can damage the forest floor, so be careful and use paths where possible.

LOGISTICS

Participants are divided into even groups (pay attention to the even division of males/females, as the physical strength of the teams should be balanced). After the introduction/motivation each team is assigned their off-road car – a set of four tractor tyres. Their task is to complete the whole track with all the tyres. As in the real race, teams arrive at different checkpoints along the way where they have to fulfil challenging and complicated tasks. Some of them use the tyres, some teams prefer to leave the tyres at the checkpoint, fulfil the task, return, take the tyres and carry on to the next checkpoint. Examples of the tasks are:

• short orienteering course with one of the tyres
• bridge construction over a stream
• time trial in a small river with one of the tyres
• construction of a raft and transporting tyres across a lake/river
• abseiling element
• obstacle course
• navigation via walkie-talkies (one person with the map navigates the rest of the group).

All the teams start at the same time. On certain parts of the track they run together, and then there is a central meeting place from where all the teams may go to different checkpoints. They rotate, and results from individual checkpoints are counted at the end of the game (there should be a time limit for each of the tasks). When the teams have completed all the tasks, the track continues with some more obstacles where all the teams may need to co-operate. Towards the end, there is a final time-trial, which leads to the finish of the race.

INSTRUCTOR HINTS

• The number and size of the tyres depends on the number, age and fitness level of your participants. With adults, the usual ratio is four big tyres for a group of eight participants.
• Towards the end of the game when most of the participants are very tired, encourage co-operation among the teams. The victory is not important but everybody needs to reach the finish. There should be a ceremony for announcing the winners at the end. Prizes can be handed out for the fastest team, for the most valuable person in the whole race, fair-play prize, and so on.
• You can mix some instructors among the participants during this activity. They can become role models for the fair play and motivation. Also, participants realise that the instructors are willing to take up the same challenges.
• The tyres can be very dangerous once they get out of control, especially running downhill. Introduce strict rules for the tyres – nobody can be positioned lower than the tyres on a slope. If necessary, in difficult parts of the track the tyres can be taken up/down one after another.
• Estimate the level of physical fitness of your participants carefully and adjust the length of the track. If the game takes too long (over four hours), it can get very exhausting and you may need to think about refreshment stops along the track.

INTRODUCTION/MOTIVATION

If possible, get the promotional video from the real Camel Trophy competition (or four-wheel drive event) and show it as motivation. It often happens that participants start to believe that they will really get to drive the off-roaders!

POSSIBLE MODIFICATIONS

All the tasks between the checkpoints can be modified. Use whatever is available.

3 Finnish Trail

Author:	Petr Holec
Social emphasis:	M
Physical emphasis:	H
Creative emphasis:	L
Psychological emphasis:	L
Preparation time:	2–3 hours
Instructors for preparation:	4–5
Material needed:	ropes, harnesses, karabiners, stopwatch, tyres, logs and various natural materials and objects
Duration of the activity:	2–3 hours
Number of instructors for activity:	4–5
Number of participants:	15–30
Location:	outdoors
Time of the day:	daytime

GAME OVERVIEW

Physically demanding game with a team element involving trust and communication. The task is to overcome all obstacles on a course and to finish as fast as possible.

SETTING

Obstacle course set in an outside natural setting. The running part does not need to be long (approximately 1.5 km), but the course should include several quite difficult obstacles. For example, low/high-ropes elements, flying fox, jumping into water from substantial height, rock-climbing or abseiling, crawling through a pipe, and so on.

LOGISTICS

- The game is usually introduced as a relay race with approximately four to six participants per team. Other members of the team can support their colleague who is currently on the track, offer advice, and so on. The next runner can enter the obstacle course only after the previous one has finished.
- For obstacles which are too challenging for some participants, there should be a substitute task, such as additional running (which should time-wise be less advantageous than taking the obstacle itself).

INSTRUCTOR HINTS

- Give participants who are unable to take part in the game a role on the track (cheerleaders, taking care of the drinks, and so on).
- All safety standards for individual obstacles need to be followed.
- If there are water activities included in the game, make sure that participants do not stay wet for too long.
- Make sure that participants take enough liquid – the game is physically quite demanding.

4 Mountain Golf

Author:	Ota Holec
Social emphasis:	M
Physical emphasis:	H
Creative emphasis:	L
Psychological emphasis:	L
Preparation time:	2 hours
Instructors for preparation:	1
Material needed:	tennis balls, material to mark a golf course (sticks with numbers, paper ribbons), golf clubs (which can be made by participants – sticks with no sharp ends)
Duration of the activity:	1–2 hours
Number of instructors for activity:	2
Number of participants:	8–30
Location:	outdoors
Time of the day:	daytime

GAME OVERVIEW

Team competition inspired by the atmosphere of a golf tournament. Involves fitness, team co-operation and fun. The task of the team is to go around the whole golf course and place the ball into all the holes.

SETTING

Varied countryside, possibly with a stream. There is a golf course prepared, with holes made by cutting the bottoms from plastic bottles and digging these into the ground. The course runs through difficult places (across a stream, through some rocks, and so on). The holes can be put in easy spots, such as meadows, but some can also be in quite tricky places such as a hollow stump, or on top of a little hill.

LOGISTICS

Participants are divided into groups of five to nine. Each person is assigned a team place (first, second, third, and so on), which they keep throughout the game (depending on the number in the team). Players use the (self-made from dead tree branches) golf clubs, and the number of clubs per team can be regulated. The goal is to place the ball into all the holes in a given order. You may only use the clubs to strike the ball. Throwing or moving the ball with any other part of the body is not permitted. The only exception is when the ball is in the hole, and the team can then take it out, place it next to the hole and strike it with the club in the direction of the next hole. The players take turns according to their number. Nobody can hit the ball twice in a row. It is possible to hit the ball any time; that is, when it is still moving. Once it stops, it cannot be shifted to any other place. Likewise, the terrain around cannot be altered (branches moved away, stones pushed aside, and so on).

INSTRUCTOR HINTS

- This game is also successful with lower age groups (10+). Then you should have one instructor guiding each team to make sure participants do not get lost, count the score for them, watch for safety and keep spirits high during the game.
- If the game is introduced as a competition (and all teams start at the same time), bear in mind that there can be collisions at the holes. State the rules before the game starts. For example, each team gets one hit, then they need to step aside and let the other team(s) have their hit, taking turns until one of the teams is successful and leaves the hole.
- It is also possible to start half of the teams in the opposite direction on the course.
- Golf clubs can be potentially dangerous objects. Make sure that everybody is aware of this.

POSSIBLE MODIFICATIONS

- The goal can either be for the team to reach the end first or to count the number of hits (as in real golf). The dynamics are very different in each case.
- If you want to make the whole game more of a social/fun occasion, you can get participants to wear costumes (men, hats and ties; ladies, scarves) and introduce some appropriate social conversation/terms on the topic of golf.
- There is also a night version of this game. In this case you need to shorten the course significantly, preferably keep it on open spaces, meadows, and so on, and mark each of the holes with a red flashing bike light. Also the balls need to be painted bright colours, otherwise they will soon get lost in the dark.
- For a smaller area, flags can have points written on them (10, 7, 4, 2...), which can be torn off and collected. Teams can choose in which order to go to each flag. No holes are needed and points are scored when the ball touches the flag.

5 Princess Shin-Sho

Author:	Antonín Rosický, Jiří Walder, based on *Night Passenger* by Allan Gintel
Social emphasis:	H
Physical emphasis:	H
Creative emphasis:	L
Psychological emphasis:	M
Preparation time:	3 hours
Instructors for preparation:	1
Material needed:	stretchers, detailed maps of the area, compasses, ropes, 2 canoes, head-torches, train time-table (possibly walkie-talkies or mobile phones)
Duration of the activity:	4 hours
Number of instructors for activity:	2
Number of participants:	25–45
Location:	outdoors
Time of the day:	evening/night

GAME OVERVIEW

Strategic/physical team competition. Two teams carry one of their members on stretchers, transport him/her in the train/on a boat, and finally return to the starting point.

SETTING

Sparsely inhabited countryside with a river and a railroad track. The teams move on paved or unpaved roads through the countryside; the distance covered depends on the strategy of each individual team.

LOGISTICS

Participants are divided into two competing groups. These need to be balanced in terms of physical fitness, leadership strengths and also in terms of male/female ratio. Teams are introduced to the layout of the whole track and to the detailed rules. The main activity is to take an injured 'Princess' on a stretcher along a given track through points A to F (see Figure 10.1). There are a number of sub-tasks to be fulfilled by the team in order to win the race. The task is to bring the Princess to the finish, plus the stretcher, boat and all the carriers (participants), and also to solve a crossword. The Princess cannot touch the ground during the whole journey. Any other forms of transport, apart from those mentioned, are forbidden.

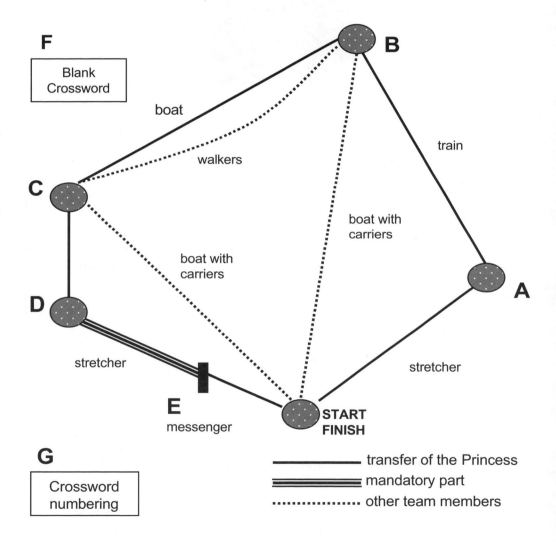

Figure 10.1   Princess Shin-Sho plan of the track

For each part of the track there are specific instructions:

- Starting point to A – The Princess is carried (distance 5–7 km).
- A to B – The Princess goes by train. The stretchers are folded, the Princess needs to be carried into and out of the train. From there the train leaves at a given time to point B.
- B to C – The Princess is transported on a boat. The stretchers are folded and placed in the boat. There are two guides travelling on the boat with the Princess.
- C to D – The Princess is taken to the beginning of the mandatory part of the track.
- D to E – Mandatory part of the track, where both stretchers (and accompanying teams) must follow a given track.
- Apart from carrying the Princess along the given track, the team needs to obtain a blank crossword, which is hidden at point F, and the numbering of the crossword, which is hidden at point G (see Figure 10.1).

It is up to the teams how they organise themselves and how they use their individual members. There must be carriers for the stretchers, carriers who bring the boat to point B and from point C, someone to bring the blank crossword and someone to bring the crossword numbering. Other roles will appear during the game as new, unexpected situations arise. There are several controls during the game. The reason for these controls is that the teams should stay in close contact during the whole game. Otherwise they could lose motivation. The controls are:

- Both of the teams must take the same train – most likely there will only be one at that time of the day.
- The crossword plays an important role in the game. The vertical clues for the crossword are contained in a letter carried by one Princess, the horizontal clues in a letter with the other Princess. The letter can be opened first at point C, after the Princess has left the boat. The winning team therefore needs to leave one of its members behind to wait for the other Princess so they can get the other clues.
- When the winning team gets to point E, there is a messenger waiting for them with a letter, which says: '*The Princesses are being transported on the wrong stretchers. Stop the escort and go back with the empty stretcher on the road between points E and D. Exchange the stretcher with the other team. The other team is not allowed to obstruct the exchange.*' It is important to mention at the beginning of the game that a messenger with an urgent message will appear at some point, so the winning team does not have the feeling the instructors are pointlessly slowing them down. This opportunity gives the losing team a chance to catch up with the winning team. There may be other controls, but these should not impede the progress of the winning team. The finish of the game can still decide everything.
- It is important to stress at the beginning of the game that in order to win, teams have to have all the members and objects and completed crossword at the end. It often happens that one team finishes, ready, but one or two members are missing – or the crossword is not solved. At that moment, the second team comes in and takes the victory!

INSTRUCTOR HINTS

- The rules of the game can be modified/simplified according to the goal of the whole activity in your course and/or according to the natural surroundings. If there is no navigable river available, the boat can be replaced by a heavy log, for example. It is important, however, to keep the overall aim of the game – to manage a complex team task, including physical demands, spread over a large area, under time pressure.

- It is important to applaud the performance of everybody, especially of the losing team. After three or four hours of action, it can be very disappointing not to receive any recognition.
- It is a good idea to leave the review for the next day. Everybody can get some rest and also emotions will settle.
- Make sure that your time planning is good. Too much or too little time can ruin the game. Both teams need to make it to the train station on time because if one of them misses the train, the game is over not only for them but also for the other team, as they will not be able to exchange the stretchers, and so on.
- The Princesses (participants on the stretchers) need to be suitably dressed because they will not be able to move for several hours.
- Do not choose a road where there is traffic.

INTRODUCTION/MOTIVATION

It is 1959. Chinese soldiers enter Lhasa and the only chance for a seriously ill Tibetan Princess to escape is to be transported along a difficult track to a hospital on the other side of the mountains in Nepal. The rescuers have to carry her on a stretcher to catch the last train to the mountains and then continue the most difficult parts of the journey by boat. The Princess can only enter the hospital with a solved crossword, which testifies that she really is a Tibetan princess. There are many of the most able Tibetan young people who want to serve her majesty and save her life...

POSSIBLE MODIFICATIONS

The track can be adapted according to natural conditions around your base. Any of the strategic elements can be replaced but make sure that things still hold together logically if you decide to replace some of them.

6 Sitting Game

Author:	Světla Horáková, Lucie Vondráková
Social emphasis:	M
Physical emphasis:	H
Creative emphasis:	L
Psychological emphasis:	L
Preparation time:	2 hours
Instructors for preparation:	1
Material needed:	paper ribbons to mark the trail
Duration of the activity:	30–60 minutes
Number of instructors for activity:	2
Number of participants:	14–30
Location:	outdoors, varied countryside
Time of the day:	daytime

GAME OVERVIEW

Team competition involving physical fitness, team co-operation, bonding and fun. The task for each team is get to the end of a track as fast as possible by changing the places where participants sit.

SETTING

A track, up to 1 km long (can be shorter) – carefully chosen. Part of it can be on a nice flat surface, such as a meadow, but do not be afraid to lead it through some mud, a stream, or undergrowth.

LOGISTICS

Participants are divided into two/four teams. All team members sit next to each other, their hips touching each other, in a 'log' line. At the start of the game the last member of the group stands up, runs to the front of the group and sits, their hip again touching the next person.

Only when this person is seated can another person from the back of the team stand up and move the same way... and so on. The task is to cover the whole distance in this manner. The team that gets to the finish first wins.

INSTRUCTOR HINTS

- If there are more than two teams, teams may obstruct one another. Check if the track is wide enough, or start another pair of teams in the opposite direction.
- It is necessary for the teams to have their direct competitor, going in the same direction, otherwise the game can easily lose its dynamics.
- It is a very good idea to have instructors playing with each team. It helps at the beginning of the game to keep spirits.
- It is necessary to inspect the track for any sharp objects before the game (or dangerous plants or animals, if that is the case in your country).
- Participants should not be wearing any watches or jewellery.

11 *Creative Games*

It was a very colourful time full of new pictures… I like and enjoy thinking back on it and always trying to bring some of those widespread colours into my life.
International course participant

Chapter overview

The following games are presented in this chapter:

1 Colour Mass
2 Dead Poets Society
3 Improvised Drama
4 Land Art
5 Pointillism
6 Rehearsal of the Orchestra
7 Wag the Dog
8 Web Pages.

1 Colour Mass

Author:	Jaroslav and Jitka Jilemičtí, after Swedish inspiration
Social emphasis:	M
Physical emphasis:	L
Creative emphasis:	H
Psychological emphasis:	M
Preparation time:	1 hour
Instructors for preparation:	1
Material needed:	water-based non-toxic paint, large sheets of paper, water, plastic sheets to protect tables/floor from paints, natural objects (stones, sticks, pine cones, etc), sheets of A5 paper/card, paper frames, scissors, glue stick, string, pegs, music
Duration of the activity:	1st part: 30–45 minutes; 2nd part: 30–45 minutes
Number of instructors for activity:	1
Number of participants:	5–30
Location:	anywhere
Time of the day:	any time

GAME OVERVIEW

An art workshop to develop creativity. Participants randomly spread colours on big sheets of paper and then look for interesting/beautiful details and create little pictures.

LOGISTICS

First participants cover large pieces (or roll) of paper with paint. It can be introduced with an exercise/practice in mixing/blending colours without brushes, reminiscent of childhood finger-painting, using natural objects, sticks, cones, stones, and so on, but mainly their hands and fingers. The goal is a colourful, abstract and fully covered sheet of paper.

The second part of the game takes place when the colours become dry. Each participant gets two L-shaped pieces of paper, which form an improvised picture frame. The task is to walk around, inspect the paintings closely and find interesting/beautiful details. The paper frames can help to form the boundary around the picture, to experiment with the size of the picture. Chosen details are then cut out and pasted on white pieces of A5 paper/card to create a real frame/picture. They can name the picture and write this name under the picture. Finished pictures are hung on a display line with clothes pegs or paper clips. At the end there may be an 'opening of the art gallery' where the artists can introduce their pictures.

INSTRUCTOR HINTS

- Stress that it is not necessary to be a real artist to be successful in this game. Essentially, enjoyment is important, not the result.
- For the first part to be successful you need an abundance of water-based primary colours (blue, red, yellow).
- Use the paints depending on the type you have available. They should not be too runny as it may ruin the pictures and may take longer to dry (this may also apply if weather is cold and wet, or the layers of paint are too thick). There may be another activity in between the two parts.
- Choosing smaller pictures (frames) often produces the best results.
- Warn the participants that they may (and most likely will) get dirty. They should wear something old and dispensable.

POSSIBLE MODIFICATIONS

- Four or five participants can be seated around a large sheet of paper and paint a certain topic together, using colours to express, say, feelings, challenge, adventure, life, and so on.
- The artists can give their pictures names or titles, or the other observers can guess the name. There can also be an auction at the end where the pictures are sold for various services.
- On PDP courses, it is often used in connection with company values. Clients look for details that correspond with the values.
- It can also be used as a special way of debriefing the whole course or as an individual activity. Participants look for details which express the most important thing they have learned or are taking home with them. Then the pictures serve as a tangible memory of the course.

2 Dead Poets Society

Author:	Gabriela Steierová
Social emphasis:	L
Physical emphasis:	L
Creative emphasis:	H
Psychological emphasis:	H
Preparation time:	1 hour
Instructors for preparation:	1
Material needed:	pens, paper and candles
Duration of the activity:	2–2.5 hours
Number of instructors for activity:	1
Number of participants:	10–30
Location:	indoors/outdoors
Time of the day:	evening

GAME OVERVIEW

A creative poetic evening activity. Participants write poems inspired by words. Inspired by the film *Dead Poets Society* (1989) starring Robin Williams. Creative aim: breaking inhibitions, opening new channels of creative expression.

SETTING

Location is inside/outside with quiet, pleasant atmosphere. Participants sit in a big circle. There are candles (one for each participant) and slips of paper on which inspirational words are written. Examples are:

belief, fortune, eyes, bridge, secret, fire, mood, evil, destiny, sound, path, dream, roots, hands, love, heaven, birth, sense, comfort, stars, key, relief, home, curse, rest, night, light, mirror, journey, joy, hope, cage, tree, rain, sea, time, earth, rainbow, message, water, door, clouds, dawn, snow.

LOGISTICS

After a short introduction each participant chooses one word (the one they feel attracted to, they like, or feel is important for them) and writes a poem inspired by that word. The time for writing is approximately one hour. After that, participants gather again in the circle and read their poems out loud. After the course, there can be an almanac published including all the poems.

INSTRUCTOR HINTS

- What is/is not a poem? – Introduction should include a short passage encouraging participants to write as they feel. Poems do not have to have rhymes, rhythm or any particular shape. What is important is the inner content, the true expression of one's feelings.
- International courses – participants can write in their own language.
- During the writing, participants can leave the group area and find their own private comfortable place. After the time limit, they are called back by, for example, the sound of a flute or bell.
- Aim to keep a pleasant, open, receptive atmosphere. This can help those who are shy of reading their poem in front of the others. If some are not willing to share, it is OK.

INTRODUCTION/MOTIVATION

Scene from the film, readings from different poems or verbal improvisation by the instructor.

3 Improvised Drama

Author:	Unknown
Social emphasis:	M
Physical emphasis:	M
Creative emphasis:	H
Psychological emphasis:	M
Preparation time:	none
Instructors for preparation:	1
Material needed:	CD player, blindfolds
Duration of the activity:	1–1.5 hours
Number of instructors for activity:	1–2
Number of participants:	10–30
Location:	indoors/outdoors
Time of the day:	any time

GAME OVERVIEW

Improvised role-play and creativity.

LOGISTICS

The workshop can consist of many different improvised exercises, which should progress from the easier to more difficult ones to give people time to relax and feel free to express themselves. It also depends on the creativity and skill of the members of the group and their age.

The following activities can be used during the improvised drama:

1 Warm up – pretend to pass an object around the circle (no talking)
   – hot potato
   – chewing gum
   – broken old egg
   – feather, and so on.
2 String – make something from a piece of string.
3 Katrin and Torsten – two groups approximately 1–2 m apart lying on stomachs or backs or with heads together. One group is called Katrin, the other Torsten. The instructor tells

a story: if Katrin is mentioned, the members of the Katrin group chase Torsten members; if they touch someone, they include them in their group – and vice versa. The group being chased runs to a safe zone, and then the game and story continues as above until everyone is in one group.

4 One, two, three, turn – one person, the observer, stands with their back to the others, who are gathered on the opposite side of the room. Observer counts '1 – 2 – 3' as the rest of the group slowly creep up towards them. On the count of '3', the observer turns suddenly and if they see someone still moving that person needs to go back to their starting position.

5 Relaxation – imagine you are:
   – a tree in the wind
   – a cat lying in the sun
   – standing under a (cold/hot) shower and slowly stretching
   – standing on a rocking boat
   – climbing to the peak of a mountain
   – lifting a heavy box onto a shelf
   – elastic that stretches and then releases
   – a spinning doll that slowly stops and then falls down
   – a puppet being pulled up/down
   – a jack-in-the-box – a clown coiled in a box that is opened
   – walking normally and then pushed back by a very strong wind.
   Then in pairs:
   – carrying a glass window and standing it up against a wall
   – carrying a ladder
   – carrying a heavy table
   – walking under an umbrella while it is raining.

6 Group frozen pictures – the group present a scene, which can be moving at the beginning with people talking. The instructor then asks the group to freeze. This is then a snapshot of the scene and should be without talking. The instructor then introduces the next scene. Scenes could include the following:
   – tram full of people
   – family on a trip
   – queue for tickets, tickets sold out
   – lovers and envious people around
   – football stadium
   – waiting room at the dentist
   – robber in a shop
   – heavy metal band
   – wedding ceremony
   – animals on the farm.

7 Moving pictures – in two groups creating one big machine with many parts and sounds, with each person being one part of the machine.

8 Dialogue in pairs – two people create a dialogue according to the roles given and the starting words below. They are given a few minutes to prepare and the dialogue can be open-ended or just one sentence.
   – 'Come here...'
   – 'Why should I?'

      – 'I want to tell you something...'
      – 'And what?'
  Roles for the different actors:
      – two robbers
      – married couple after 20 years
      – mother and son
      – teenage girls in their late teens.

9 Reading a newspaper text in a certain way (after a few minutes to prepare)
      – as a speech at a funeral
      – cheekily
      – formal speech for an audience
      – happily
      – drunkenly
      – self-consciously.

10 Mirrors – non-verbal, in pairs/fours (just face and hands). Pairs face each other; one is the original, the other the mirror. One makes slow gestures/actions that are reflected in the mirror.

11 Sculpture (in threes) – move from one position to another. Create three different poses – on a signal make position one, then slowly move to the second and then to the third.

12 Sculptures (in pairs) – one person creates a sculpture from their body; the second, who is blindfolded, tries to find out what this sculpture is and copy it.

13 Group sculpture – make a sculpture of two people, then four... until everyone is part of it.

14 Expressing emotions connected with entering a door – one person rings the bell; second person opens the door. As the door is opened both react in a pre-decided emotional state (scared, happy, excited, bored, depressed, surprised, astonished...).

15 Group collaboration
      – Move in space in any way you like.
      – Start observing others, form pairs mirroring one another's movement, moving in the same way.
      – Then combine to make groups of three or four moving in the same way.
      – Gradually the whole group makes contact, moving in the same way, expressing friendship, cohesion and togetherness.
      – Repeat procedure but this time the atmosphere is hostile/tense.
      – Repeat, but now everyone is scared, astonished, relaxed, lethargic, happy, scared.
      – Repeat with music, first individual and then dance with others in the group. Respond to the change of music.

INSTRUCTOR HINTS

- This activity should be in the first part of the course, but not at the beginning.
- Give them the chance not to participate in some part if they wish. Do not push them; do not let them leave if you feel they could join later on.
- Give yourself time to close it (small debrief at the end and/or one in the middle).

4 Land Art

Author:	Bob Stránský
Social emphasis:	L
Physical emphasis:	L
Creative emphasis:	H
Psychological emphasis:	M
Preparation time:	none
Instructors for preparation:	none
Material needed:	pictures of land art for motivation
Duration of the activity:	2–4 hours
Number of instructors for activity:	1
Number of participants:	10–30
Location:	outdoors
Time of the day:	day time

GAME OVERVIEW

Creative activity, concern for and appreciation of surroundings, landscape, environment and nature, and developing works of 'land art' directly from inspiration and natural material resources available.

SETTING

Land art works best as a relaxed, fairly slow activity where participants can relax after a demanding activity, spend some time on their own or in a company of someone they have chosen themselves.

LOGISTICS

After the introduction, participants divide themselves into small groups (up to four people). They then wander around, find interesting locations, let themselves be inspired and create a piece of art. The time for this creativity must be clearly specified (1–1.5 hours). After completion, a gallery is opened. Participants walk around, artists introduce their works and specify angles from which their pieces should be seen, and so on. Other participants can make up titles for a particular piece, comment on it in any way, reflect and take pictures.

INSTRUCTOR HINTS

- Try to choose an inspirational place in the countryside (nice, interesting views, enough suitable material, and so on). The activity can bring amazing and varied results on beaches, in forests, among big rocks, in vast meadows, and so on.
- Stress at the beginning that no damage to nature is acceptable; that is, no felling of living trees, no cutting big branches off trees, and so on.
- The final works should not be judged, but rather appreciated as they are. It is not a competition, but a peaceful interaction with the natural environment.

INTRODUCTION/MOTIVATION

A human being came up from the earth, was formed by the landscape and only much later started to transform the landscape. At the beginning it was only footprints on the beaches, later there were the first paintings in the caves – all these marks showing the unique human existence. Man was bound by nature and its laws for a long time. In sharp contrast to this is today's surprisingly arrogant attitude towards nature. We are still very dependent on natural resources – and these actually enable us to escape nature and its elements.

Land art is a way to get back to nature. It is an art form, which originated in the 1960s and 1970s. As opposed to earlier art developments, it does not use any high-tech materials, is not trying to surprise by its technical perfection or stunning colours. The ideal of land art is a piece of art created by a human being, but in such a way that it does not disturb the landscape; it belongs to the scenery, adds something to it, does not obstruct or interfere with it and does not pollute it either. Examples are piled up stones, shells, sand, driftwood and other natural materials that make a shape on the beach. Each tide slowly damages and disintegrates the creation. Other artists work in the open landscape using non-conventional materials – grasses, or flowers. It is the process of creation, not the result, which becomes important.

5 Pointillism

Author:	Jitka Mikšíčková
Social emphasis:	H
Physical emphasis:	M
Creative emphasis:	H
Psychological emphasis:	M
Preparation time:	1 hour
Instructors for preparation:	2
Material needed:	water-based non-toxic paint (no black), 2 × 2 m sheets of thick large paper/card, tape, model pictures to be reproduced – colourful paintings with figural or concrete motifs (e.g., Gauguin, Matisse, Van Gogh, Klimt, etc.), lively music, boom box.
Duration of the activity:	1–2 hours
Number of instructors for activity:	1
Number of participants:	10–30
Location:	outdoors, flat safe terrain for bare feet
Time of the day:	day time

GAME OVERVIEW

Dynamic and creative team game involving running and painting. Teams create large works of art in the pointillist style by transporting paints on various parts of their body. Connection of two principles: physical activity and creativity; using both brain hemispheres (reason/analysis and intuition/emotion) for completing the task.

SETTING

'Studios' and 'canvases' can be set up in a line on a wall (or something similar) with a flat grassy/concrete area in front, allowing enough space for each group to gather, or in a circle amidst trees. The studio (one per group) has a place for the colours and is marked by a rope/chalk approximately 10–20 m from the canvas. The canvas (one per group) should be approximately 2 × 2 m, thick, large paper/card taped on a wall or tied on a tree. Make sure that the paper is stable and thick enough for painting dots on it.

LOGISTICS

Participants are divided into teams of five to seven members. Each team gets/chooses a picture. The task is to reproduce that painting in large scale in the pointillist style. The new painting should resemble the original painting as much as possible in terms of colour shades, proportions or shapes. After the introduction, time is set aside for colour mixing. The only way to paint is using *'dots, dot, dots...only dots'*. No lines are permitted on the canvas. Paints need to stay in the studio all the time. They can only be transported on designated parts of the body (thumb, big toe and nose). Usually the painting time lasts 10 minutes, then there is a three-minute break, when all the participants need to stay in the studio and use this time to plan how to continue the painting. At the beginning of each new painting section the painting technique is announced. At the end, there can be an official opening of the gallery, when groups introduce their works of art and take pictures.

INSTRUCTOR HINTS

- The game requires large amounts of paint. The paints need to be water-based and non-toxic.
- Start with only one part of the body, say thumbs, being used for painting, otherwise the canvas will be completed too quickly. Use or add other body options for the next periods.
- Choose the location and clothing carefully. In the course of the game participants are likely to paint on everything and everybody.
- Lively music brings lots of energy and fun into the game. Keep the boom box a long way away from the running crowd and away from the paints.
- Instructors can also take part, to help break the barriers between the two groups.
- Remember that washing after the game will take quite a long time. This is another interesting group experience if you use an outdoor hose!
- The area for the game needs to be carefully inspected, as participants will most likely run barefoot.
- Suggested points for assessment: artistic impression, technical neatness (no running colours), similarity to the original, new approaches, interpretations, and so on.

INTRODUCTION/MOTIVATION

One/two instructors dressed as artists are painting pointillism pictures for the annual 'Paris Saloon' (exhibition of the best paintings).

Painters in their studios are preparing for the annual 'Paris Salon' – exhibition of the best new masterpieces. Modern painting is different, no longer lines and shapes... there is a new method 'Pointillism'... where you can paint just dots, dots, dots, dots... Your studios will transform classical paintings into the new pointillism style.

POSSIBLE MODIFICATIONS

The course of the game and approximate time schedule is as follows:

Time (mins)	Action
• 5	Dividing participants into teams
• 15	Introduction, explaining the rules, demonstration of how to paint

- 2   Each group chooses one picture to paint, pointillism style
- 10–15   Strategy time for the groups
-             Start the game by a whistle and shout 'sketching time'
- 40–60   Painting and reflection time (see the time schedule below)
- 10   The end – photos, presenting the masterpieces
- *extra 30–60* *Spontaneous body art, washing in the outside showers.*

A possible structure of the painting time schedule is as follows:

Method of Painting	Time (mins)
• Running – painting with thumbs	10
• *Reflection in the studio*	3
• Running – painting with noses	10
• *Reflection in the studio*	3
• Hopping – painting with big toe	10
• *Reflection in the studio*	3
• 'Wheelbarrow' – painting with big toe of the wheelbarrow person	10
• *Reflection in the studio*	3
• 'Piggy back' – painting with noses + big toe of the carried one	10
• Finishing	10

6 Rehearsal of the Orchestra

Author:	Milena Holcová
Social emphasis:	H
Physical emphasis:	L
Creative emphasis:	H
Psychological emphasis:	L
Preparation time:	1 hour
Instructors for preparation:	1
Material needed:	costumes, different props, lots of paper, paint, old bed-sheets or fabric, script of a theatre play (optional), spotlights, sound system, musical instruments
Duration of the activity:	8 hours – 1.5 days
Number of instructors for activity:	1
Number of participants:	15–30
Location:	indoors and outdoors
Time of the day:	day time

GAME OVERVIEW

Managing large project under time pressure, team co-operation, creativity and fun. Participants rehearse a theatre production and perform it in front of a real audience.

SETTING

The hall/stage for the performance should be in some little town or at some festival so it is possible to attract an audience. A performance can also be done in a nursing home, children's summer camp, and so on.

LOGISTICS

One day before the performance (preferably in the evening) participants are introduced to the whole project. Their task is to divide roles (director, costumes, musical director, stage manager, props, promotion, and so on), rehearse a theatrical performance and the following night perform on a real stage in front of a real audience.

Most of the participants will have to have more than one role in the preparation part and should also have some acting role in the performance itself. Participants can work on the piece during the night (if they so choose) and the following day in the morning. In the afternoon they need to move into the performance venue, and rehearse again. Additionally, at the same time, promotion is necessary to attract an audience – small sketches done in a local square, posters, personal invitations, short spots on local radio stations or anything else appropriate. The climax comes with the performance itself. After that, there can be a festive dinner prepared by the instructors to celebrate the success.

The choice of the performance can either be made by the instructors (choose something where there are many actors on stage so everybody can participate, possibly a fairy tale) or it becomes a part of the decision making of the participants. They could also write, direct and perform their own story.

INSTRUCTOR HINTS

- The hall/stage should be booked well in advance, usually before the course even starts. It is possible to arrange the performance at some amateur/alternative/music/art festival or add it to any other big social gathering. In this way it is possible to show the participants posters which promote their performance even before they have actually started working on it!
- Instructors should stay in the background. They can help with getting the material, preparing the stage, and so on, but they should not play the major roles in the performance.
- It is a good idea to run a meeting with the participants or the director a couple of hours after the project has been introduced to see how they are doing, what they are going to perform and how. This meeting gives the instructors a chance to help out with sensible suggestions concerning the organisation of the whole project. This way you can make sure that the whole thing develops appropriately and that the performance will be really successful.
- This activity should only be used towards the end of the course. It is a long and intensive project, which requires a lot of communication and co-operation between participants. The performance can be the climax of a course – it is difficult to carry on with a normal programme afterwards.

7 Wag the Dog

Author:	Bob Stránský, Jožan Šebesta
Social emphasis:	M
Physical emphasis:	L
Creative emphasis:	H
Psychological emphasis:	M
Preparation time:	1 hour
Instructors for preparation:	2–3
Material needed:	2–3 video cameras with video cassettes, TV and VCR, costumes, art material (papers, paints, and so on), flipchart
Duration of the activity:	4 hours
Number of instructors for activity:	3
Number of participants:	15–30
Location:	indoors and outdoors
Time of the day:	day time

GAME OVERVIEW

Activity involving creativity, team co-operation, strategic thinking, flexibility, trying out new unusual roles and fun. Two competing teams produce TV news spots, create 'media reality' and thus influence public opinion on the presidential candidates. *Wag the Dog* is inspired by a film (1997) of the same name by Barry Levinson. Motto: 'Why does a dog wag its tail? Because it is smarter than the tail – if the tail was smarter, it would wag the dog.'

LOGISTICS

Instructors nominate two leaders for the groups – these leaders choose their teams, which become creative-production teams of experts (one supporting the President, the other the Foreign Minister). Their task is to create media reality, win political potential from the situation and gain the victory for their candidate in the elections. Their task is to create TV spots for the News, revealing new information which enhances their candidate (and/or discredits the other candidate). There are five days to the elections. The first day lasts 45 minutes (each following day is 5 minutes shorter: 40, 35, 30, 25 minutes). At the end of the day (that is, the time which the teams have for producing the items) there is the TV news where all the spots are shown. The PLUS MINUS Agency (the instructors) then decides on the credibility, that is impact, of the spots and releases the latest opinion poll statistics (there is a detailed graph on a flipchart, which documents the flow of support throughout the game). The new day begins at the end of the broadcast. New spots are developed for Day 2. On Day 5 elections are held, and the Main Press Agency releases the results (that is, the instructors decide, after the last round, which of the teams was better at persuading the public about the suitability, credibility and merits of their candidate.)

Rules for the spots
- Teams are not allowed to use any well-known figures, real or true events.
- Candidates cannot physically be present in the spots – their faces never appear on the screen. All the news reports are just about them.
- The maximum length of each spot is 3 minutes.
- All controversial information (for example, allegation against allegation) is verified/denied by the Main Press Agency (the main umpire of the game – the instructors). It is the only authentic source of information.

INSTRUCTOR HINTS
- Teams should assign specific roles to individual members (cameraman, director of the spots, costumes, analyst, strategist, timekeeper and so on). According to need, all members can become actors in the spots.
- Make sure at the beginning of the game that all the cameramen know how to work with the camera. Remind them of the basic rules of shooting because the quality of the spots is important (sufficient light, quiet surroundings so one can hear what the actors are saying, beware of too fast swings or zooms).
- The changes of public opinion are important factors, which can significantly influence the game. The instructors, who decide on the poll swings, need to be careful to stay neutral. It is also good to give a brief explanation as to why this has happened (the candidates actions are logical, credible; voters are influenced mainly by XYZ, and so on).
- Should the game start slowly and the teams are not too sure of what to include in their spots, it is possible to introduce more information into the game via the Main Press Agency: a sudden earthquake in the southernmost part of the country; the visit of an important statesman from a neighbouring power; negotiations about the state budget for next year, and so on. Be careful to choose neutral information, which will not favour one of the candidates.
- If there are any sensitive topics in the current political situation of your country, do not mention them in the game.

INTRODUCTION/MOTIVATION
TV news: *We are reporting from a small village not far from the summer residence of the President. Today, early in the morning, a car accident has been reported. In a 'hit and run' incident, a speeding car knocked down an elderly lady who is currently in hospital with serious injuries. In spite of this, police were able to question her. She remembers that the car was dark green. An eyewitness who we managed to find in the village reported the same.*

Interview with the witness: 'I went to walk the dog, suddenly I saw this... bit further down this road... dark green colour, it was a luxury car, I tell you... there was a big bang, well, I saw it only from the distance... no, I ain't gonna say more, I don't want to get into trouble... Stop it! Don't shoot it...'

Our crew managed to find out what type of car is used by the President during his stay in the summer residence. As you can see, this car has not been driven on the paved roads of our capital [a shot of a dark green car splattered by mud]. The spokesman for the President has not yet made any statements on this matter. This event could influence public opinion and affect the President's position in the upcoming elections. His continuation in office is not certain. This situation considerably enhances the position of the other presidential candidate, the former Foreign Minister.

The end of the President's mandate will certainly be the most difficult moment in his career. According to the poll of The PLUS MINUS Agency the chances of both candidates are even at the moment. There are still five days till the elections and most of the experts are not able to estimate which of the candidates the voters will choose in the end. Part of the electorate will go for the President because of the economic growth our country has experienced during the last couple of years. Despite that, his popularity has gone down from 69 to 43 per cent. His rival, the former Foreign Minister, is gaining more supporters as the call for change is intensifying. Moreover, his moral credit, international contacts and recognition among the foreign political elite make him a strong candidate for the presidential position. His popularity has increased steadily – from 24 to 37% during the last couple of weeks. The last moments before the elections will decide this thrilling duel. Both candidates will fight for the last 20 per cent of voters who have still not made up their minds. We remind you that in this presidential system, which leaves strong authority in the hands of the President, we are deciding on the future of the whole country. Therefore each voter has the right to know everything about the candidates. We will keep you informed.

POSSIBLE MODIFICATIONS

Teams of participants can work on various projects:

- short advertisement spots (on PDP courses they can promote their own company or some of its products)
- video clips to various songs
- short sketches commenting on events on the course.

The particular type of project depends on the type (and length) of the course. It is always great fun and it can be used as a preparation for larger drama projects towards the end of the course. It is also possible to organise an Oscar show as a follow-up to this activity where various prizes are awarded (Best Actor, Best Actress, Best Movie, Best Costumes, and so on). Such an activity can serve as a big social occasion.

8 Web Pages

Author:	Bob Stránský
Social emphasis:	M
Physical emphasis:	L
Creative emphasis:	H
Psychological emphasis:	M
Preparation time:	20 minutes
Instructors for preparation:	1
Material needed:	paper, envelopes, old newspapers and magazines, pens, rulers, scissors, glue, sticky tape, coloured pencils, water-based paints, staplers
Duration of the activity:	1.5–2 hours
Number of instructors for activity:	1
Number of participants:	10–30
Location:	indoors
Time of the day:	any time

GAME OVERVIEW

Creative workshop making paper collages in the form of personal web homepages which characterise their owners. Aim: getting to know each other, creating space for further communication among participants.

LOGISTICS

Participants meet in a room where all the art material is prepared for them on tables. They pair up and become clients and web designers. In pairs, their task is to create homepages for each other, using materials (old newspapers and magazines) which are available for them. The page should include their name, something that characterises them (where they come from, their hobbies, what they like, their job, and so on). Each homepage needs to have an envelope attached to it – this envelope later becomes a 'mail box', which is used during the whole course for participants' private communication. The pairs need to communicate verbally during the activity and find out as much as possible about the other person, so each can create as accurate a homepage for their client as possible. At the end, all the homepages are hung up at the local 'intranet' (a net of strings attached to a wall). Each person can then introduce themselves as well as their page. After the activity is over, encourage the use of the 'net' for participants to write letters/messages to each other throughout the duration of the course.

INSTRUCTOR HINTS

- Make sure after the activity that there are always pens and pieces of paper available by the net so everybody can write letters to the others.
- Usually instructors have their own envelopes on the net, so participants can also write to them.

INTRODUCTION/MOTIVATION

You may play a sketch of two people trying to meet in the Internet, a chat room full of people who know nothing about each other, and so on. A more formal introduction is also possible. Bolster creativity among participants – there are all sorts of crazy things on the net!

POSSIBLE MODIFICATIONS

- The system of writing letters to each other can be used even without the process of making the homepages, as a sort of private feedback which participants give to each other. Then instructors just hang out the envelopes with the participants' names on them and ask everybody to write personal letters to whoever they want to say something. This writing is usually done just before the end of the course and results in each participant travelling home with an envelope full of feedback from the others. This envelope is only opened after the course is over – as a reflection of the course.
- The style of creating homepages can be modified according to the material and resources you have available. Make sure that there is enough material for everybody to work at the same time (such as glues, scissors), or divide participants into two groups, each working at different times.

12 *Psychological (Reflective/ Emotional) Games*

An environment that encourages different emotions to come out... is a key factor in personal change; if you feel comfortable with how you feel and with expressing it, you are more willing to keep that change going.

International course participant

Chapter overview

The following games are presented in this chapter:

1 Games without Borders
2 Labyrinth of the World and Paradise of the Heart
3 Mars Venus
4 Nexus VI
5 Night Images
6 Stalker
7 Triffids.

1 Games without Borders

Author:	Jana Matějková, Bob Stránský
Social emphasis:	M
Physical emphasis:	L
Creative emphasis:	M
Psychological emphasis:	H
Preparation time:	1 hour
Instructors for preparation:	1–2
Material needed:	recordings of ethnic music, tape recorder, and candles
Duration of the activity:	2–2.5 hours
Number of instructors for activity:	2–3
Number of participants:	15–30
Location:	indoors
Time of the day:	evening

GAME OVERVIEW

Introductory and emotional activity to meet, communicate and break barriers with others. An evening based on world music, real and imaginary greeting rituals of different cultures and non-verbal communication.

SETTING

Participants move freely around a room that is decorated in a way to create a pleasant atmosphere. The specific greetings presented by the instructors are mainly fictional, but be aware that for some participants these greetings could appear to be real.

LOGISTICS

After the short introduction/motivation the instructors start with the first greeting. Each greeting is briefly described with a made-up story and then demonstrated by the instructors. Music corresponding with the particular greeting plays in the background. After each history, participants mingle and greet each other. For each of the greetings, there should be enough time afterwards to meet several people (approximately 5–10 minutes). The instructors monitor the atmosphere and estimate when to introduce a new greeting. Depending on the type of music available, the greetings can be adjusted, omitted or numbers increased.

INSTRUCTOR HINTS

- Instructors should actively be involved in the game as it helps to overcome any initial shyness.
- It is good to have one instructor to operate the music and two others to introduce the greetings.
- The activity can affect participants quite deeply – especially when people are open and take it seriously. A sensitive ending to the game is necessary, as well as some free time afterwards. No other activities should take place that night!
- This activity is very culture-sensitive. Before introducing it, carefully assess your participants, how accustomed they are to being touched by others, how intimate can you go. Lots of barriers can be broken down, but you need to prepare participants slowly and gradually. Start with moderate touches (accompanied with a humorous comment).
- The introduction is important to set the atmosphere. If a participant starts feeling uneasy, it must be possible (and publicly acceptable) to step out of the game. They must be able to choose the intensity of the interaction with individual people.

INTRODUCTION/MOTIVATION

Welcome on our journey around the world. Tonight, we are going to visit different nations, people, and places on our Earth. We are going to find out how these nations greet each other. We are all familiar with the European tradition of shaking hands, but even here we can find some differences. So let's start our journey, visit different cultures and try out their greetings. Try to use all your senses when you meet other people, but do not speak.

GREETINGS

France

A small double-kiss on each cheek, but in reality more like putting cheek to cheek.

The French greeting was originally developed by the local women who used to be carefully watched by their men. This type of greeting gave them a chance to whisper to each other secrets which they did not want to share with their men.

Africa

Feeling each other's head, hair and face.

In Africa, there are many tribes and all of them have different shaped heads and hairstyles. Sometimes they meet in total darkness and there is no chance of finding out whether or not the other person is from your own tribe other than feeling their head and hair.

Peru

Back-to-back rubbing, sort of a back massage.

Many of the people in Peru live in high mountains who work as sherpas and carry heavy packs on their backs. When they meet, they want to relieve their tired backs so they put away their packs and rub their backs against each other. In this way they can give each other a nice massage.

Greece

Palms on each other's heart, looking into each other's eyes.

This greeting takes us to Greece and symbolises a warm heart and good intentions. We place each other's hands on the heart, look into each other's eyes, stay like that for a moment and then we can introduce ourselves by name.

Tibet

Placing ears next to each other and listening.

In Tibet, people are very spiritual and they try to listen to their inner voice. When they meet, they try to hear the soul of the other person. What they do is to bring their ears slowly close to each other and listen at length.

Ancient Ireland

Standing back-to-back, arms lifted, touching and interweaving with arms of the other person. Move as trees and tree branches in the wind, swing in the wind, intertwine hands as branches.

Ireland is the land of Celts and their priests were called Druids. In the past these men used to have a very close connection with trees; they considered them sacred and admired them. Their greeting resembled trees, waving and intertwining their branches. When they met, they stood back-to-back, lifted their arms and stroked each other, danced in the wind, waved hands and greeted each other in this way.

Cuba

Smelling the scent of the other person (on arms and around neck).

The people in Cuba are famous for growing the best tobacco in the world and for making the best cigars. To be able to distinguish all the types of tobacco, they need to have very sensitive noses and they use this ability when greeting people. When they meet somebody, they try to smell them. They start at the place where the neck meets the shoulder and then they slowly follow the arm all the way to the hand and back.

Inuits, Māori of New Zealand

Gently rubbing noses.

Noses are important for other nations, too. They were used for Eskimo or Inuit greetings. Where Eskimos live it is quite cold so they need to warm their noses. When they meet each other, they rub their noses against each other. A very similar greeting is used in New Zealand, the 'hongi'. There they touch foreheads while pressing noses twice. At the same time they breathe out through the nose, which is a symbol of sharing the same air. In this way, Māori people from different tribes could share 'the breath of life' which protected them against evil spirits.

India

Touching with foreheads.

The little dot that we often see on Indian people between the eyes on the forehead can symbolise the third eye. With this eye they try to see the essence, the substance of the other person, their inner self, to see what is hidden inside. When they meet, they look into each other's eyes, slowly bring their foreheads together and interconnect their third eyes.

Atlantis

Listening to the heartbeat of the other person (standing or sitting position).

This was a Dream land, which we are not sure really existed, but a legend has it that the people who lived there were very sensitive and open to each other. They wanted to get in touch with the inner self of the person. Therefore when they met each other, they did not want to talk but rather listen to the other person's heart. They found a position which was nice and comfortable for them, and tried to listen to the heartbeat of the other person.

China

Sit opposite each other and touch each other's feet and legs.

Many people in China spend day after day working in the rice fields. Therefore their feet become very sensitive and they use them when they greet other people.

Back home

We are coming back home to our own countries. We can greet people in your own natural way. Hug each other or find the way which you think is most appropriate.

POSSIBLE MODIFICATIONS

There are two versions, depending at which stage in the course you want to use the game:

- Days 1–3: introductory game, meeting other people, getting to know each other. Greetings are lighter, and the pace is faster.
- Days 6–10 (not at the very end of the course!): participants know each other already, now they have a chance to interconnect on much deeper levels. Greetings are longer and can be more intimate.

2 Labyrinth of the World and Paradise of the Heart

Authors:	Jana and Tomáš Ledvinovi, Vojta Svoboda; adapted by Světla Horáková
Social emphasis:	M
Physical emphasis:	L
Creative emphasis:	M
Psychological emphasis:	H
Preparation time:	4 hours
Instructors for preparation:	1
Material needed:	Map of the Labyrinth, paper with 'autobiography', pen and journal for each participant, sufficient amount of various coloured cards (one colour for each checkpoint), backpack for each participant, load for their backpacks (bottles of water, wooden logs, bricks, etc.), sound system, music, material and equipment for individual checkpoints (see below), material for the handicaps (blindfolds, 'white sticks', bandages, crutches, possibly wheelchair), gong or bell, tokens for money (could be made of paper), costumes for instructors, papers, pens, paints, glues, etc.
Duration of the activity:	3–5 hours
Number of instructors for activity:	5 (preferably more)
Number of participants:	10–30
Location:	indoors and outdoors
Time of the day:	day time

GAME OVERVIEW

Psychological, staged, non-structured game focused on reflecting on life's choices, values, attitudes and life orientation. Addresses questions of harmony and balance between necessary and wanted, planned and possible. Players symbolically pass through stages of their own life and make various decisions in each decade. In the time between individual decades, they reflect on their decisions. Inspired by Comenius' book 'The Labyrinth of the World and the Paradise of the Heart' (new edition 1998).

SETTING

The environment of the game is divided into two parts: the Labyrinth of the World (outdoors around base) and the Paradise of the Heart (a nicely decorated room with famous quotations about life – possibly obtained from participants some time in advance – mattresses, quiet meditative music and pleasant atmosphere). On the wall, there is a big map of the Labyrinth (outdoor surroundings with marked checkpoints) and an 'autobiography'. This autobiography consists of a large sheet of paper containing names of all participants and spaces for cards, where each participant glues their 'receipts' from checkpoints visited during the individual decades. In the Labyrinth outside there needs to be space for 6–10 checkpoints, ideally up to 100 m away, symbolising the main options for fulfilling the participants' lives. All the checkpoints should express the atmosphere and the character of the particular sphere of life. It is possible to have instructors on some of the checkpoints (Family, Children, and so on), but it is not necessary. Some of the checkpoints can change as the decades pass (Work, Education), some can appear/disappear (Children). It is enough to mark the checkpoint with a short description (optionally some tasks) and leave several props there. At each checkpoint there needs to be a supply of the coloured cards – each participant takes one every time they visit the checkpoint. The whole game should take place in quiet surroundings, not disturbed by external distractions. The number and content of the checkpoints can be various:

- Water
- Work I–III: There should be some real work for participants to be done – chopping wood, carrying materials, sweeping floors, mowing grass or whatever is available. All work is paid according to the time it takes, on the participants' education (in the game, not real) and on the negotiating ability of the individuals. The work may change depending on the stage of the participants' lives. The instructors at the checkpoint may change the checkpoints' look, or change their clothes or behaviour. If the checkpoint is unmanned then changing the look of the checkpoint may also be important.
- Education I–III (school, university and learning): Changing from one to another as the decades go. There can be simple questions for participants to answer, such as passages from books to be learned by heart, tests to be completed. Schools may charge some money for education (depending on the tradition of your country). It is also possible to open special courses according to the wishes of participants – such as driving courses, creative writing, accounting, and so on – of course for an appropriate amount of money. Once again the instructors may change their clothes or behaviour depending on the stage of the participants' lives.
- Relationships, old family (parents), new family (children): It starts with parents – young people visit them, talk to them, can ask for money (or give money to their parents), help with some work, or just simply hang around. During the game, parents get older and die (family checkpoint can be replaced by a little grave with a photograph) and a new family is established with the participants' own children.

- Hobbies, travelling (I–III): Area with maps, travel guides, pictures from exotic places. All trips need to be paid for.
- Leisure time, entertainment (can be put together with Hobbies): music, concerts, cinema posters, sports, exhibitions, gardening, and so on.
- Helping others, charity work, friends: This checkpoint is to communicate with the other people in the game, talk to them, share, and so on.
- Spirituality, inner life: Meditative music, philosophical books, sets of questions leading participants to search for meaning in what they do.
- Hospital: Place where some of the diseases, handicaps and illnesses can be cured, usually for money. Not all of them are curable, though. A special card (Health) is distributed here for each decade. If stopped by Destiny, one can show the card and it protects from diseases.

LOGISTICS

The Labyrinth of the World is the actual content of life, which is chosen and created by man (the participant). There are several checkpoints placed around the Paradise of the Heart, which symbolise the main spheres of activities – studies, work, family, friends, pastimes, inner life, and so on. Participants enter the Labyrinth and choose how they spend the time assigned to the given period. Sometimes Fate thwarts their plans and they have to cope with its inroads. Paradise of the Heart is the inner dimension of man – here everybody reflects silently on their decisions, wishes and desires; assesses and plans further steps. They also write down what they have been through in the form of a journal or letters to special people, and so on. It is a private confession, which stays hidden from the others.

MAIN ROLES FOR INSTRUCTORS

- Fate (black-and-white costume, mask): Fate moves freely through the Labyrinth and Paradise and at times interferes with people's lives (for example, those who work all the time get a heart attack). This is done in the form of stickers with names of diseases/handicaps, and/or real handicaps (blindfolding people, tying their legs together, putting little stones in their shoes, and so on). Sometimes participants may draw 'luck/handicap' cards from a hat, but beware the atmosphere when handing out the handicaps – fatefulness must radiate, not malevolence.
- Angels: Destiny's assistants (one dressed in white, one in black, with masks): They fulfil Fate's assignments, observe participants, decide together with Fate about the handicaps and other interference (marriages, good and bad news, and so on). Towards the end of the game, they bring 'Death' by blindfolding the person and carefully leading him/her to Paradise. They are stern and impartial.
- Helping hands: They try to be as invisible as possible. They help where needed and change the checkpoints when participants are in the Paradise of the Heart.

The game is introduced without explaining the rules. The environment – the Labyrinth of the World and the Paradise of the Heart – provides the rules, as in real life. The only instruction participants receive is in the speech of the 'Father' before they are born.

Decade 0–10 – Paradise of the Heart: The participants are woken up earlier than usual and asked to prepare to be 'born' in a few minutes (with sleeping bag, backpack, pen and journals if they have them). They should lie down with eyes closed and can fall asleep again in the main room (this is a good time to decorate the Paradise of the Heart) or alternatively blindfolded participants are brought to an already decorated room sometime during the day. Birth happens when the blindfolds are removed. Fate, together with the Angels, is present and they help the participants to get up. The game starts with the 'birth' of participants into a New World.

Labyrinth of the World: The decision to leave the 'heart' should be left to the participants and from there they move through life. Their main guideline is the Labyrinth of the World plan. The participants are set free into the surroundings of the base and explore. They can go to each checkpoint, get to know them or execute their set tasks (as they reach the appropriate age) and they receive cards for their autobiography. The participants can choose which checkpoints they will visit and in what order. They must not forget to have a drink of water, which symbolises the ability to care for themselves – to ensure basic life needs. Their first decade outside will not be too long (10–15 minutes) enabling a few visits (school – first grade – and parents). A gong or bell announces the change to the next decade. The players return to the room and record their experiences and meditate over their future. The same kind of relaxing music should play every time they are back. Each decade lasts approximately 10–15 minutes. Each break in the Paradise of the Heart lasts 5–10 minutes.

Decade 10–20: The players go again to the Labyrinth. They learn how to orientate themselves in the world. They are getting to know 'life' and start to understand what the game 'life' is about. They start to be motivated, and to get to as many checkpoints as they can in the next decade in order to start to live a full life.

Decade 20–30: Into the third decade (and at the beginning of the fourth) everyone receives a symbol of age (two full water bottles, and a wood log in a backpack...). This symbol will make movement in the Labyrinth of the World more difficult, so the players will be forced to make a choice. Now they know where the individual checkpoints are, they set out to fulfil their resolutions. They can start to work. Then there is marriage and children (marriage is symbolised by a string, which ties the hands of partners together). Fate and the Angels set up the couples from those who put their name on a special piece of paper headed 'Some time in my life I would like to get married.' Not all who want to get a partner will get one; some couples get divorced after a while. Children are symbolised by a wooden log, which parents need to carry with them all the time. Some participants may become single mothers/fathers.

Decade 30–40: Some more may marry or divorce. Some may receive a handicap as a symbol of illness/accident (handicaps: a blindfold over one/both eyes; one arm tied to the body; tying legs, inserting little stones in their shoes; need to walk barefoot, crutches, and so on). One or two participants can be told that they have an incurable illness and that there is only a couple of years before they will die (illnesses are symbolised by a sticker with the name of the disease, which participants wear on their clothes).

Decade 40–50: In this decade everybody has some sort of restriction (disease, handicaps, and so on). New things happen (for example, the death of parents in the form of a letter from a relative), first grandchildren can be born, problems of getting a well-paid job dependent on their education).

Decade 50–60: Handicaps are getting harder (all participants have some load in their backpacks – they need to carry more for each decade). First participants die. They cannot enter the Labyrinth anymore and cannot communicate with those who are still alive. Preferably they stay completely silent, in their own reflections.

Decade 60–70: Retirement, less money, more people staying alone and more people dying.

Decade 70–80: Loneliness (very heavy loads in their packs), and then the last participants die. Everybody is back in the Paradise of the Heart. Leave pleasant music playing (the same as at the beginning).

The money, which they earn by working, can be used to pay the hospital bills where the doctor can cure small problems, but does not usually heal big illnesses. The doctor also charges quite a lot of money. They can be asked to pay some money for food, university education or wherever it is appropriate (travelling, hobbies, entertainment). During the first two decades they can get some money from their 'parents' to be able to pay before they actually earn some money.

Fate can enter the game and reacts to the players' behaviour. For example, if someone only works and has no time for family relationships or holidays for a long time, that participant gets a 'heart attack'. The player can also become ill with an incurable illness and have only a limited number of years to live. How will their behaviour change?

INSTRUCTOR HINTS

- This game is one of the most complicated and difficult to run. The preparation is quite complex and the co-ordination during the game must be agreed on before the game starts. There needs to be an instructor with psychology/therapy training and preferably somebody who has seen/played/introduced the game before.
- Encourage participants to be creative. All the instructors at the checkpoints need to be ready to improvise and to try and fulfil the wishes of participants. 'Parents' can behave as real parents (sometimes they lend money, sometimes they borrow money from their children); employers can negotiate, sometimes be biased, as happens in real life.
- The game needs to have a carefully chosen place in the scenario. It cannot come earlier than Day 4 in the course, but should not be introduced just before its end; there would be no chance for instructors to check on their participants.
- The game can disclose sensitive topics within participants. Observe, watch their reactions and behaviour, and intervene when necessary. It is good to know the background of the people (family problems, deaths). The game brings totally different results for 18–30-year-olds, as they tend to try to live their life in the present. For older adults, age 40+, it is often looking to the past. It is not recommended that you play this game with children under 18.
- All instructors should read the introductory 'Father' speech and have explained to them the sense and structure of the game. Give them all the information, which will give them a picture and understanding of what is happening.
- Choose instructors you feel would fit the particular checkpoints, or ask them before what they prefer, and discuss it with them. Give them the responsibility to prepare their stand, to think up the content of the place and how it should change with the ages of the players. They need a sign for their checkpoint, and coloured cards for the receipts. Give them enough time so they can think about their role and prepare for it (at least half a day) before the game starts.
- The debrief should be the same day, but a while after the game finishes. Some instructors, especially those who play the main roles (parents...), should be available to talk to participants if required. It is good to know where they are and what they are doing in case some of the participants need their help. There may be a lot of emotions displayed during this life game and it is possible that there will also be some at the debrief. Some people find it easier to share personal things in smaller groups. Possible topics: parallels between the

game and real life; forgetting/adding something to their real lives; planning/chance; harmony and balance between possible and wanted; accepting old age, dying.

INTRODUCTION/MOTIVATION

The 'Father' speech:

Even before you are born you are already in the Paradise of your Heart. Outside there is a whole world waiting for you and this world is a Labyrinth of different challenges and obstacles. There is also success and happiness to be found. You will go into the world but will always return to the Paradise of your Heart where you are able to find true peace, love and understanding, along with the answers to all questions. You will explore the Labyrinth of the World. After being born you will go into the Labyrinth several times. Each visit will be the equivalent of a 10-year period in your life. It is up to you to decide how you will spend this time. The choices are Work, Education, Hobbies, Spiritual Journey, Parents, Your Own Family and Partner. Each time that you enter the Labyrinth you must go to the Hospital and take a card (Health) there. Health is vital for your life in the world out there. As a symbol of satisfying basic human needs, you must drink a glass of water. Water is vital, as without it there is no life. All the rest depends on your choice.

The bell [or other appropriate sound] will call you from the Labyrinth of the World back into the Paradise of the Heart where you can think on the decisions you have made in the last 10 years. Take a moment to write your thoughts and feelings into your journal. You can write a letter to your friends and family at this time. You could explore the questions that you had no immediate answer to during this period. It is a time to make plans for the next journey into the Labyrinth and decide what you wish to achieve in the next 10 years. The bell will ring and send you on your way to the Labyrinth again. You will spend all your life travelling between the Labyrinth and the Paradise of the Heart.

The moment of your birth is close. After you have been born, you will start living the first years of your life. Once you have enough strength as a child you can enter the Labyrinth for the first time.

POSSIBLE MODIFICATIONS

- In this game, it is more important to understand the essence of the game; how it is actually executed, is not so vital.
- If you start the game early in the morning, it is possible to include breakfast into the introductory part before participants go to the Labyrinth for the first time. It looks like a children's breakfast, participants lying still in their sleeping bags, instructors in costumes, bringing some toys and food, playing with the 'children', feeding them, acting out the parents' role.
- There is a lot of flexibility in how the individual checkpoints will be arranged. If you do not have enough staff, organise them so they do not require the presence of an instructor.

3 Mars Venus

Author:	Unknown
Social emphasis:	M
Physical emphasis:	L
Creative emphasis:	L
Psychological emphasis:	H
Preparation time:	20 minutes
Instructors for preparation:	1
Material needed:	candles, motivational quotes about male and female character and behaviour, and so on
Duration of the activity:	2 hours
Number of instructors for activity:	2 (one male, one female)
Number of participants:	15–30
Location:	indoors
Time of the day:	evening

GAME OVERVIEW

Discovering and sharing opinions about relationships, one's own sex, on the other sex; trust building in the group, emotional team bonding. Learning to be open and sharing in a safe environment, learning about oneself and others. Do men talk and share in a different way from women?

SETTING

Male and female participant groups have separate times during the game to discuss the same topics. There is always one group sitting in a small circle around a few candles in the middle as the only light (with an instructor of the same sex), talking on the given topic. Participants of the opposite sex create a bigger circle around the smaller one, they can only listen and observe; they cannot interrupt the discussion in the inner circle. The atmosphere should be relaxed, open and intimate.

LOGISTICS

Instructors choose two or three main topics they want to concentrate on during the activity. For each topic, there is a separate round, with the male and female groups having their turn in the inner circle to discuss the set subject (approximately 20 minutes). The instructors decide when the groups should change places again and also when to open another topic. A sketch, a short story, a personal experience, a quote or just a simple question can introduce each topic. Participants can also react spontaneously to something they have heard in the group of the opposite sex. Possible topics for discussion would include:

- typical characteristics of the sexes – are there male/female behavioural reactions to particular situations, and so on?
- abilities – what things are women better at than men?
- everyday life – division of labour in the household, equal pay, and so on
- friendship vs. relationship
- long-term and long-distance relationship vs. someone else available now and here.

INSTRUCTOR HINTS

- The topics for discussion presented by the sketches should be chosen carefully to suit the group. You can find inspiration in life or in books; for example, *Men are from Mars, Women from Venus* (Gray, 1992). The sketches are meant to be short and focused. Be comfortable and reasonably unbiased with the topics you are presenting, as this activity is influenced by the way it is introduced.
- Some topics may be quite provoking in some cultures; others may not be interesting if they are subjects commonly discussed in public. Think about your participants and their culture before you choose the topics.
- Age group is vital for the choice of the subject matter. Teenagers perceive different topics as important and interesting from older participants.
- It can be a very emotional activity, so expect to be involved with the discussions, otherwise the game may lose its magic.
- Facilitate the discussion sensitively. The discussions should be long enough for everyone to give their opinion. However some people are not comfortable to share with a large group and are happy to be listeners. Respect their choice and do not provoke them into discussion.

POSSIBLE MODIFICATIONS

This system of discussion can potentially be used for any topic, which should be chosen because it is interesting, surprising, or an eye-opener for the listening group.

4 Nexus VI

Author:	Jaroslav Jičínský, Martin Šťastný
Social emphasis:	H
Physical emphasis:	H
Creative emphasis:	L
Psychological emphasis:	H
Preparation time:	2 hours
Instructors for preparation:	2
Material needed:	personal computer, floppy disc for each group, head-torches, pens, paper, various material for decorating the room, disturbing music/sounds (hooter, industrial sounds, and so on), identification labels, sticky tape
Duration of the activity:	4 hours
Number of instructors for activity:	3 + 1 for each participant group
Number of participants:	12–30
Time of the day:	night, early morning

GAME OVERVIEW

Game inspired by the film *Blade Runner* (1982) by Ridley Scott. Physical, psychological and self-reflective aims involving extremely demanding run, vain 'journey to gain immortality', and reflection on one's life in the perspective of finality.

SETTING

Dark night/early morning, 'industrial setting/futuristic factory' (room covered with plastic, foil or similar), possibly stroboscope. Outdoors, running on paved as well as unpaved roads, heading towards an old quarry, half-destroyed house or any other desolate place. The running circuit should be 5–15 km (1–1.5 hours), depending on the fitness level of your participants. Atmosphere in the group should be intense; participants should be alert and running quite fast.

LEGEND OF THE GAME

There is a group of androids (robots) coming to the Earth. They are known as 'Nexus' and are basically machines made by man to execute specific tasks, carry out hard work and so on, but they look exactly like people. Somehow it happens that these machines gain human feelings too, and start to behave like humans. They gain consciousness and they start to want to live forever. This threatens people, who send out special units (Blade Runners) who are supposed to eliminate all the androids. Androids are trying to find Dr Tyrell, their creator, who is the only person who can guarantee their immortality. It is a race – they need to find him before the Blade Runners eliminate them all.

LOGISTICS

Before the game starts, the instructors divide the participants into groups of five to eight people related to their running/physical ability. The instructors then assign each participant a serial number (for example, NEXUS 6-532/M), where the last alphabetic character determines their membership in the given group (Group 'M' or Group 'X'). Participants are woken up abruptly in the middle of the night (approximately three or four hours before dawn) and each assigned their serial number. Then they gather in the 'industrial room', which symbolises a space ship. An on board computer announces that they are all androids and soon they will land on Earth. Also the group divisions are announced (this allows the androids to be more mobile and have a better chance to escape the attention of Blade Runners). One instructor accompanies each group. Everything is under stress, everybody needs to leave the room quickly and start hiding because Blade Runners could be anywhere.

When the groups leave the room and start on their journey, the instructor running with each group must stop at a hidden spot and explain the situation again, repeating the rules, and clarifying their own role. The instructor also plays the role of a Nexus-guide who has been on Earth a long time so knows where to go and what to do. The task of each group is to get to the house of Dr Tyrell who invented and constructed the androids. He is the only person who knows about their past, why they are here, and how they can gain immortality.

Most of the journey should be on a paved surface where the group can move fast, running most of the time. Blade Runners could be driving cars passing by, so the group needs to hide in ditches or behind trees or any place available. There are other Blade Runners on the way too – instructors in cars or just walking by, trying to spot any moving groups. If the group does not hide in time, a Blade Runner can take one of their members away and 'put them to sleep'. If it is not clear who the Blade Runner actually saw moving, the group has one minute to decide which member will be sacrificed. The instructor acting as Nexus-guide is not there to help or comfort them, but just a guide who can 'punish' anyone who endangers the group. Their task is to keep the group moving fast and show them the way.

The groups of exhausted replicates come to the house where they meet Dr Tyrell (for example, each group will run for a minimum of 45 minutes to get to the house. The faster groups are given longer routes so they run a lot further to get there and back). There they receive the following information:

I am Dr Tyrell, your creator. Information about your life and death are top secret and cannot fall into the wrong hands. Therefore I have encoded all the information onto four floppy discs, which are here in my house. You can take ONE of the four parts [depending on how many groups you have in the game] back with you to the space ship and decode it together with the other replicates. It is easier to escape the Blade Runners in smaller groups so you can only re-unite with the other androids back in the space ship. There all the information will be revealed to you. Time flies and the end is close. Do not forget! Hurry!

The journey back is as fast as possible. The group may run back using a different route, possibly using a track another group has been using – they will meet but need to hide from each other, as the approaching group may be Blade Runners. They need to be able to carry the floppy disc containing the information all the way to the space ship. All the groups meet back where the game started. One after another, they put their floppies into the computer to put together the vital message from Dr Tyrel. At this moment, those replicates who were 'put to sleep' during the game should be brought in so they can hear the message.

> *I, Dr Tyrell, leave the world an invention, a humanoid robot of the type Nexus VI, and the following four-part message:*
>
> *1. I would like here to comment on the speculation claiming that the robot Nexus VI can live several times longer than man. Yes, it is true Nexus VI androids can live for up to five times longer than man. Because of the fear that the long life of the androids could turn against man and man could be in the hands of replicates, I decided that all robots should have the microchemical life limiter, which spreads to the neurone system after four years.*
>
> *2. To those who doubt this and claim that there exists a way to stop this decay, I would like to say that the organism of the replicates reacts to any attempt at prolonging its life by mutation which is complete within 10 minutes of this occurring. There now remains less than a year of the type Nexus VI.*
>
> *3. All replicates who hear my message please stay in the space ship, and during the course of the next 10 minutes try to list in a few sentences how you will use your final year – what you want to achieve and experience. You may programme the recording of your plans into the space ship mainframe, which will put them into the memory banks of the other androids.*
>
> *4. It is, however, important to say that even this step is classified as an instigation of mutation and will prolong departure for rest. I wish you courage in the searching and granting of your hopes and plans. I regret that the immortality of the type of life that you are seeking does not exist.*
>
> *With regards from your creator, Dr Tyrell.*

After the message is heard, everybody (including the instructors acting as Nexus-guides) gets pen and paper and has a couple of minutes to formulate what they want to fulfil, experience and do in the course of this last year of life. All the messages are put into a box. When they have all been collected, each person takes out one message (not their own) and reads it out loud. After reading the last message, the game is over.

INSTRUCTOR HINTS

- Watching the film *Blade Runner* before introducing the game may help instructors understand the background of the activity.
- The game is logistically extremely exacting because after the game has started it is not possible to communicate with other members of the instructor team. You must have agreed on all the details of the game's proceedings, roles of individual instructors, and so on, before the start. Also, all the group's Nexus-guides need to agree on the way they are going to behave towards participants so they all gain similar experience during the game.
- All the instructors guiding the groups must be familiar with the routes they are going to take. They cannot get lost and there is no time to consult a map in the middle of the game.

- There needs to be a set time limit when all the groups meet back at the space ship. Too long spent waiting for some of the groups can ruin the atmosphere. Instructors running with the groups must do everything possible to keep to the limit and be there on time.
- Each participant group can lose up to four members. It is not good to create an atmosphere suggesting that the Blade Runners will get everybody sooner or later, as it lowers the motivation to run and finish the game. Only those who are not careful or lucky enough are put to sleep on the way.
- Those participants that are caught and put to sleep are blindfolded and transported back to the centre. There they are 'stored' in a dark, quiet room with no information and they are not allowed to speak to each other. They rejoin the rest of the runners when the groups come back from their journey.
- The game should finish at dawn. As participants are up for most of the night, it is a good idea to give them time off (to rest, sleep and relax) until about 11 a.m. and do the final debrief before lunch.
- This game can be emotionally disturbing, as a result of participants' strong physical performance bringing them to the edge of exhaustion, coupled with the questions of life and death, mortality and limits of human life. It requires experienced instructors, and at least one who has had psychological training and is able to intervene in the case where somebody gets too far from their comfort zone.
- Safety must be considered carefully. Participants are required to run in darkness, not always on paved roads. There is a certain level of risk in this which cannot be diminished, but careful inspection of the circuit during daylight before the game can inform the instructor of possible dangerous places. Carry first aid kits and mobile phones.

INTRODUCTION/MOTIVATION

LA, 2073 AD. A group of replicates (androids) is coming to the Earth in a stolen spaceship. They have violently managed to escape from one of Jupiter's moons – Io – where they worked in ore mines. The reason for their escape was their hunger to know the truth about their origin, destination and possible immortality. At the same time they want to get closer to the human race, find the meaning of their lives, and thus became immortal. They will not be stopped by anything. During the searching operation, Blade Runners were activated. These are special forces trained to search for replicates and their task is to find them and put them to rest.

POSSIBLE MODIFICATIONS

If you have a group of participants on the course who for any reason cannot run, it is possible to create a special group which does not cover the whole distance, and to organise a nearby place where they can obtain their part of the message. However, this needs to be done with great caution, so as not to spread around the idea of a disabled group. All the rest of rules remain the same for them, such as being chased by Blade Runners, hiding in the ditches, and so on.

5 Night Images

Author:	Allan Gintel
Social emphasis:	M
Physical emphasis:	L
Creative emphasis:	M
Psychological emphasis:	H
Preparation time:	none
Instructors needed for preparation:	none
Material needed:	candle
Duration of the activity:	1.5–3 hours
Number of instructors for activity:	1 per group
Number of participants:	6–8 per group
Location:	indoors/outdoors
Time of day:	evening

GAME OVERVIEW

Discussion activity, where participants compare each other to different objects and thus express their characteristics in a figurative manner. Reflective aim, giving each participant a chance to learn something important about themself.

SETTING

Location is quiet and undisturbed by others. Each group sits around a candle. The introduction/motivation (see below) induces a serious, but at the same time, intimate atmosphere. Emphasise that none of the information shared will be discussed anywhere else, and invite participants to be honest, open and frank.

LOGISTICS

The game has three rounds. Round 1, the candle is placed in front of one person in the group. They select an object/thing which should be used as a comparison in the description of their personality. Example: *'What would I be like if I was a road, a house, a car, a book, a month in a year, a landscape, a tree, a film, a colour...?'* The others consecutively answer from their point of view. The described person listens. Round 2 is where the other participants choose an object or thing that, to them, describes the person. They should try to expand on their answers with, if necessary, reasoned explanations. Again in this round the described person only listens. Round 3 everybody describes themself as above.

INSTRUCTOR HINTS

- The game should be used only after participants have had a chance to get to know each other quite well; that is, towards the end of the course, but not at the very end!
- Introduce basic rules of feedback before the game starts; participants express only their own personal views.

- Encourage participants not to say only '*It would be a stony road*' but to add, for example, where the road leads, who uses it, how often, and so on, so that the image can give the described person some message/information about themselves.
- The instructor should also take part in the game; it helps the atmosphere and makes it more open. The instructor should guide in an informal, sensitive manner, discreetly regulating the speed.

INTRODUCTION/MOTIVATION

A: '*Listen... we will make a test. Sort of a game. Think of a woman.*'
Uncomprehending look.
B: '*Just any woman?*'
A: '*No, the one you know best.*'
He started to get the idea. He looked at me.
B: '*And you?*' *he asked.*
A: *I nodded.* '*Me too. And I ask the questions.*'
There was only dim light in the room. When I leaned back, there was shade on my face. It was like the past... and present?
How she lies.
A: *Carelessly. If it matters a lot to her, she puts more effort into it. Always knows to whom she lies.*
B: *Reluctantly. She feels offended. She feels offended by the fact that she knows she will have to lie. Despite of that she will do it.*
You without her.
A: *Working.*
B: *I do everything with the feeling that she is some place.*
Her grace.
A: *In what she used to be at the beginning.*
B: *Her changeability. When she looks like a lady and wears a childlike expression.*
Her letters.
A: *Neatly written, long, kind. She is no poet.*
B: *Beautiful, so true that it almost hurts.*
As a caretaker.
A: *Very bad, she would not last long.*
B: *Perfect. She would hand out keys. She would be interested in everything happening in the house.*
What would she be if it were a building?
A: *Constructivist building from the 1920's, practical and nice, well built.*
B: *A bottle of red wine. Tart and tasty. Sorry, that is not a building. Classical cathedral. No ornaments, functional, marvellous...*
There was smoke and bit of a vanilla aroma from tobacco in the room.
A: '*Did you talk about Stephanie?*' *I asked.*
B: '*Yes.*'
A: '*That is weird,*' *he said in thoughts,* '*me too... .*'

6 Stalker

Author:	Milena Holcová, adapted by Jiří Walder
Social emphasis:	M
Physical emphasis:	H
Creative emphasis:	L
Psychological emphasis:	H
Preparation time:	3 hours
Instructors for preparation:	2
Material needed:	costumes for instructors (old clothes and shoes), snack packed in newspapers (perhaps slabs of bread, bacon and onion), ugly bottle with something strong to drink, two heavy metal nuts, pieces of gauze
Duration of the activity:	2–3 hours
Number of instructors for activity:	2
Number of participants:	groups of 4–6 participants
Location:	outdoors
Time of the day:	night, early morning

GAME OVERVIEW

Staged game involving a self-reflective inward journey specifying one's goal in life. Psychological and physical game inspired by the film *Stalker* (1979) by Andrei Tarkovsky. Participants go through a dangerous area towards a place where they can announce their most secret wish. On the way they reflect on their lives.

SETTING

A gloomy dawn, inhospitable and desolate area (ruins, swamps, rubbish dump, old quarries, or similar). The track does not need to be too long, but it should be demanding and create a disturbed atmosphere and apprehension.

LOGISTICS

Participants are introduced to the game at least 12 hours before the actual start, so they start thinking about their most secret wish. When they feel they are mentally ready, they put their name on a prepared list. Stalker chooses a group of people, wakes them up at dawn and takes them on the journey through 'the Zone'. Essentially this means that groups pass along a demanding track (bleak, depressing, sometimes dangerous), through rivers, swamps, ruins, junkyards, and so on. On the way, Stalker stops the group several times and asks them questions.

The figure of Stalker is extremely important and sets the tone for the whole game. Stalker is a boor, but a strong personality at the same time does not like the 'civilians' who are taken into the Zone, but Stalker needs them and is not in a hurry! The game is not about physical obstacles and dynamics, but about the internal suspense. There is uncertainty and fear in the air. Stalker is visibly nervous and is the only one who can afford to shout now and then. In the Zone Stalker requires absolute obedience. 'From now on you are all nobody! The Zone will take those who do not obey my commands immediately!'

Stalker knows the Zone and is so scared by it. A careful slow pace alternates with stampede. Any logic damages the game. There is no place for laughter. On the way the group meets the traps of the Zone, such as the mosquito glades where the danger of sinking into the ground is extremely high. Participants will be given the metal nuts, which they tie in gauze and throw in front of themselves. If the object flies straight, there is no danger and the group can move forward; if it deflects, the group has to find another way. Another obstacle is the 'witch jelly' – the only way to escape is to climb a tree, at least one metre above the ground, and stay there as long as Stalker says. Stalker has an assistant with him in the Zone – Junior. Their task is to help keep the game and the atmosphere going. They are subordinate to Stalker and do whatever Stalker wants them to do. During the journey Stalker stops several times – in places especially ugly and desolate (such as puddles, junkyards, a stream with water up to waist level). Stalker sits down there and rests, chooses a topic and asks questions. The questions are uncompromising, to get under participants' skin. Stalker's own answers show that frankness is what is interesting. 'If you kid yourselves, there is no reason for you to go any further, the waterfall [or stream] will not let you in.'

Questions could include: Why did you come to the Zone? When was the last time you were really disgusted/ashamed of yourself? What does happiness mean to you? When was the last time you felt happy? What chip do you have on your shoulder? What is the thing you cannot cope with?

Participants answer the questions one after another. With the first question, Junior answers first. Their honesty will show the others what sorts of answers are expected. Stalker should not force participants to give answers to all their questions. It is the participants who decide how much they want to share from their inner feelings. On their way, corresponding with the development of the group, Stalker changes their character and the rude behaviour slowly disappears. Before the participants encounter the last obstacle (a waterfall, or stream, or similar) which is the climax of the whole journey, Stalker can even gain some parental traits. As a consequence, participants realise that now is the hard part. The last obstacle needs to be overcome by each participant individually; nobody should know beforehand what the waterfall/stream looks like. After coming through, Stalker congratulates each participant – shaking their hand, or giving a sip from a bottle.

INSTRUCTOR HINTS

- Watching the film *Stalker* before introducing the game may help the instructors to understand the background to the activity.
- It is important to make absolutely clear at the beginning that the game is not primarily about physical exhaustion and overcoming obstacles. The main goal is first and foremost inward-looking and introspective.
- Stalker needs to be a mature and very experienced person – not only from an instructor's point of view, but also as a personality. As they ask questions about life, philosophy, and so on, they should know the answers.
- Stalker should not overplay his role or participants may over-react and become unnatural themselves. This can result in discussion which is not honest. Denying or lying is not the goal of the game!
- Stalker and Junior should have several topics ready which they can discuss among themselves in case there is a really taciturn group.
- It must be stated very clearly that all the information participants share in the group during the game will stay confidential and nobody will mention them after the game is over. The last, most secret wish will not be uttered at all – it will stay private within each of the participants.
- If there is more than one group of participants, there needs to be at least a one-hour break between them.

INTRODUCTION/MOTIVATION

A couple of years ago, shocking news appeared in the media: 'Another civilisation mystery. Question marks over our planet!' There was a reason for this – so-called 'Zones', precisely bounded areas where natural and physical laws do not exist. Entering such a Zone means almost certain death. In spite of this, there are people who repeatedly return to the Zones. Stalkers are the only ones who know the Zones; for example, where the 'mosquito glades' are – concentrations of gravity where all objects hopelessly sink to the ground. They know of 'witch jelly' – a gas which remains close to the ground and turns all organic substances to gelatine. They can avoid 'mincers' – air turbulence where all objects turn into a squeezed piece of old cloth. There are different reasons why Stalkers go back to the Zones. Some of them work as guides for sensation-seeking tourists, some just long for adventure. There is one thing all of them know – somewhere in this Zone there is a waterfall/stream of the highest value. None of the groups that have visited it have ever come back the same, yet it attracts more and more people. What is this magic attraction? What lures all those who have learned about it? Why do all these people want to experience a couple of hours of pure terror? This waterfall/stream can fulfil the most secret of all human wishes. But beware! It can fulfil only the most secret wish, not any other that we may be scared to mention out loud, that which we would not even say to ourselves, the wish that slumbers in our subconscious. It requires not only courage to step into the waterfall/stream, but also to enter the Zone. It takes courage to take a look inside one's own soul; to delve into the mind's subconscious and discover. Self-delusion will backfire.

The unique waterfall/stream allows you to enter only once. It is vital therefore to know what one really wants, as this opportunity will never occur again.

Motivation is very important with this game. It is possible to use passages from the book *Roadside Picnic* (1979) – the novel on which Tarkovsky's film *Stalker* was based, or show part of the film. If these are not available, you can use a sketch – such as dialogue between Stalker and Junior. Motivation must introduce the whole idea of Zones and the lure of the waterfall/stream. It is a good idea to enact the motivation a couple of days before the game actually takes place – it gives participants time to consider whether they really want to take part and think about their most secret wish.

POSSIBLE MODIFICATIONS

The main topic of the game can hardly be modified. What offers a lot of scope is the staging. The journey participants take and the way the waterfall/stream is pictured are all up to your discretion and the environment available.

7 Triffids

Author:	Josef Ptáček, adapted by Ivoš Jirásek
Social emphasis:	M
Physical emphasis:	M
Creative emphasis:	L
Psychological emphasis:	H
Preparation time:	2 hours
Instructors for preparation:	1
Material needed:	blindfolds, helmets, tape recorder, tape with motivation message, pleasant music for the ending, head-torches (when introduced at night)
Duration of the activity:	1–3 hours
Number of instructors for activity:	1 per group
Number of participants:	groups of 6–10
Location:	outdoors
Time of the day:	early morning or late night

GAME OVERVIEW

Psychological and physical game inspired by the film (1962) and novel *The Day of the Triffids* by John Wyndham (1986). Blindfolded teams go on a journey overcoming demanding obstacles. Aim of the game: psychological endurance, team co-operation, learning more about oneself in a critical situation, development of non-verbal communication.

SETTING

Participants are asked to wear something that can get wet/dirty (including shoes). They are blindfolded and told little about what is going to follow. During the whole game, everything should happen in complete silence. They listen to the introduction/motivation 'broadcast' from a tape recorder.

LOGISTICS

After the broadcast, participants are divided into groups of approximately 6–10. One instructor is in charge of each group and chooses one person to lead their team and their blindfold is removed. They receive information that their task is to guide the group safely and fast. The instructor will act as a guide. Their task is not to go around obstacles, but to overcome them with the whole group. The instructor assesses the level of difficulty of the obstacles. There should be a sufficient variety of them (walk through a dense forest/thicket or uneven terrain, get over/under park benches, walk through a riverbed, cross a muddy area, crawl through concrete pipes, and so on). According to the level of physical/mental fitness of the participants, you may decide to include some really challenging obstacles towards the end of the walk (walking through deep water up to the waist or even higher, even letting participants swim a short distance). The whole walk should last approximately 1.5–2 hours. As participants approach the finish, the group is split and individual members are sent (still blindfolded) to follow the sound of music, which they can hear in the distance. When they get there, they take off their blindfolds, and are welcomed by hot tea.

INSTRUCTOR HINTS

- At Outward Bound Czech Republic, participants are required to wear helmets for this activity.
- Choose leaders of the groups who appear less assertive, not so visible in the group, not willing to take over the responsibility and/or centre stage. It is also possible to change the leader and mix the order of the group during the game. It gives a different perspective when you walk right behind the sighted person rather than at the very end of the group.
- Choose interesting obstacles – be creative, and resourceful! The track does not need to be long (perhaps just around a building), and remember that the pace of the group will be very slow.
- Take any new leader well aside when explaining the rules so the rest of the group does not hear.
- The more demanding the obstacles, the more you have to watch for physical and emotional safety! Try to assess your participants, for example, people who may be claustrophobic with some of the obstacles.
- Before you debrief this activity, it is a good idea to let it sink in. It is a great team exercise, but for most of the participants it will also be a deep personal experience.

INTRODUCTION/MOTIVATION

(Best recorded on a tape with typical radio broadcasting interference)

Attention! Attention! You are listening to a special programme of the Security Council of the United Nations. We are broadcasting on all frequencies. Yesterday, during the night a new type of chemical weapon exploded in the atmosphere. The weapon was in the last phases of its testing process. A tragic consequence of the explosion is that the majority of citizens of the world have gone blind. Traffic in the world has come to a standstill. We are being flooded with news about thousands of destroyed aircraft, rail collisions and motorway traffic jams. Please do not attempt to drive under any circumstances. Roads are filled with burning cars. Houses in many suburbs have begun to burn and there are no people who can put out the fires. However, probably the greatest danger comes from Triffids, which are reported to be spreading over suburbs and rural areas. These are a new kind of plant, which until now were grown on special farms under strict control. They were grown for their multi-use in the medical industry. Besides their good characteristics, Triffids may under certain conditions be a great danger to mankind. They are carnivorous plants and feed on the meat from putrefying organisms, including man. People have gone blind and therefore have become completely defenceless against them. The Triffids kill with the aid of their long stinging tentacles and orientate themselves according to the intensity of sound around them. Unlike other plants, they are able to move with the aid of their three strong tough-skinned legs. Their reproductive abilities are almost unbelievable. So far there has been no information about how they escaped from the special farms, but we have already had the first reports of casualties. However, there are still places that are safe from Triffids such as islands in the seas. United Nations marine troops have managed to clear several islands in the Mediterranean, where groups of survivors are gathering. We ask all who can still see, who are able to move independently, to come to one of these islands and bring with them as many people as they can manage. The journey will not be easy, but it is our last chance and hope. We call on you to save mankind. We do not have much time, as the lethal plants are multiplying rapidly and the countryside is becoming more and more dangerous every minute. We implore you, do not waste time! Your fate is in your hands. Attention! Attention! For all who can hear us....

POSSIBLE MODIFICATIONS

The progress (length, difficulty) of the game depends on your goals – and the participants. A minimum of 45 minutes to one hour of blindfolded walk is recommended – usually used on our PDP courses. On long courses, it can easily become a major early-morning game, allowing participants some time off later in the day.

13 *Summary and Conclusion*

Life is not measured by the number of breaths we take, but by the moments that take our breath away.

This book provides insight into the outdoor and experiential approaches of the Czech Republic. The links between the indigenous cultures of the *turistika* activities in the Czech Republic, the concept of *friluftsliv* in Norway, and the approaches of the Māori people in New Zealand and Aboriginal people in Australia have much to offer the constructed and commercialised fields of outdoor and experiential education of Western Europe and North America.

The unique element of the VSL methodology presented in this book is the concept of *dramaturgy*, a method of course design which links, integrates and intertwines a range of innovative and creative games. During the course, instructors change the scenario to react to the needs of participants. Dramaturgy is a continuous process that ensures that the course themes provide a thread throughout the scenario. A range of games and activities is carefully sequenced to maintain a balance of intensity and rhythm. The concept of dramaturgy presents ideas for creative programming practice and its application to more holistic experiential courses.

The book offers depth and conceptualisation of these methods from a theoretical perspective and challenges the notion of established concepts such as the action/review approach of the 'adventure wave', pushing people out of their comfort zones and frontloading activities. The dramaturgy wave, pushing comfort zones in an atmosphere of physical and emotional safety, framing games in fantasy and using play in achieving educational outcomes, provides a broader and refreshing perspective for outdoor and experiential learning.

Research findings have suggested that participants may not only produce the most learning when pushed out of their comfort zones (Leberman and Martin, 2002). Qualitative findings of the effects of these programmes indicate that the *Intertouch* courses resulted in many powerful experiences leading to personal and interpersonal development that was evident up to two years after the courses (Martin, 2001d). The descriptive accounts from participants illustrated some of the images of transfer, which link the educational process and course outcomes. The key elements of the experiential education process established from these research findings are:

- an holistic course design involving a variety of activities involving reflection
- the learning environment which provides physical and emotional safety, and a positive and supportive atmosphere
- a diverse group of participants
- the instructor facilitation method.

More research is needed in the areas indicated above, using both quantitative and qualitative methods as effective ways of investigating the complex phenomena and many variables of outdoor and experiential education (people, processes and outcomes). The dramaturgy wave has illustrated social, physical, creative and reflective waves, but other waves such as environmental and cultural waves can be built into the course scenario. Using the metaphor of waves on a beach, many other programmes contain elements of these waves, but these tend to be small waves that are often crushed by the bigger waves following. The challenge is to provide a balance between the waves that provides the greatest opportunity for truly holistic experiential learning.

In summary, the course dramaturgy and range of games and activities have much to offer in terms of training of staff and course development. The methods used offer a more holistic challenge than traditional outdoor approaches in providing the next generation of effective personal and management development programmes. The approach provides experiences which challenge more people in more ways, whilst aiming to satisfy the needs and demands of both personal and management development markets, without compromising the original organisation's philosophy.

This book demystifies this Czech style of experiential programming and opens up these techniques, in English, to those experiential educators who wish to embrace the creative potential and inspiration of the Czech Way. Their challenge is to capture the essence of some of these innovative, novel and refreshing approaches, and to design their own new programmes and activities.

Appendix – Outward Bound

Kurt Hahn

'No discussion of the theory of experiential education would be complete without some recognition being given to Kurt Hahn' (Kraft and Sakofs, 1991, p.15), the German educator who founded the Outward Bound organisation in 1941. Hahn's approach to education was based on the ideas of Plato and placed emphasis on the use of experience in the development of the whole person, and the person's ability to serve the community. His philosophy is based on providing experiential education programmes that empower young people to fulfil their potential. 'Hahn was not primarily an outdoorsman. His main concern was with education in general and with the use of adventure as a broad educational tool' (Hunt, 1990, p.127). Prior to Outward Bound, Hahn had already been the headmaster and founder of two other world-renowned schools, Salem in Germany and Gordonstoun in Scotland. The motto he created at Gordonstoun was *plus est en vous* – there is more to you than you think. Hahn (1935, quoted in Richards, 1990, p.73) stated:

> *It is a sin of the soul to force the young into opinions, but it is culpable neglect not to impel every youngster into health giving experiences, regardless of their inclinations.*

Hahn's philosophy has influenced methods of training and learning for other educational institutions, school curricula and personal development methodologies. These include the United World Colleges, the Round Square Conference Schools that support community-based service learning, and school achievement schemes such as the Duke of Edinburgh Award and Expeditionary Learning. Project Adventure was set up as a direct result of Outward Bound in 1970, and the Association of Experiential Education, which publishes the *Journal of Experiential Education*, was formed from Outward Bound roots in 1976.

The philosophy of 'challenge by choice' was adopted by Outward Bound schools and enables participants to determine the level of challenge of their adventure experience. Outward Bound programmes have aimed to remain consistent with Kurt Hahn's educational principles of a balance between fitness, skill, initiative, perseverance, respect and service. Hahn's approach to education was not only experience-centred, it was value-centred.

Outward Bound International

The term 'outward bound' means 'to say goodbye to the certainties of the harbour and to undertake a journey to new horizons'. Outward Bound programmes have been running for over sixty years and currently exist in all continents and thirty-six countries at over forty Outward Bound schools around the world. Outward Bound International, an incorporated non-profit organisation, was set up in 1997 to oversee the Outward Bound schools internationally. Outward Bound International's mission statement is:

To help people discover and develop their potential to care for themselves, others, and the world around them through challenging experiences in unfamiliar settings – self-discovery through adventure.

Outward Bound is based on core values of courage, integrity, trust, compassion and co-operation. Courses incorporate the following five key components:

- Character development: Developing capacities of mind, body and spirit to better understand one's responsibilities for oneself, others and the community.
- Compassion and service: An active expression of the value we place on our common humanity, our diversity and the natural world. A heartfelt caring connection to each other and the world around us. Compassionate behaviours and a service ethic encompass both giving and receiving.
- Social and environmental responsibility: Instilling a sense of integrity that results in choices that have a positive effect on society and the environment;
- Adventure and challenge: Exciting and remarkable experiences that involve uncertain outcomes and acceptable risks, and that require special effort.
- Learning through experience: An educational process based on action and reflection. Experiences are intentionally designed, presented and reflected upon to instil values and promote skill mastery.

Comparisons with other Outward Bound schools

A number of differences between VSL and other international Outward Bound schools can be noted from both the organisational set-up (Figure A1), as well as course design (Figure A2).

Instructors/trainers from other Outward Bound schools tend to be given their course schedule by a programme co-ordinator or director. On these 'standard courses' it is seldom possible for new activities to be developed. Junior instructors tend only to observe courses until they have finished a training programme. At VSL each open-enrolment course has a unique course theme. Its programme is designed fairly independently of the office staff, as it

VSL	Traditional Outward Bound
● Unique courses	● Standard courses
● Dramaturgy method of course design	● Activity/review cycle used
● Real games and play-based activities	● Physical and group dependency
● Instructors part of the group	● Instructors facilitate the group
● Long indeterminate days	● Duration of days predetermined
● Often long working hours	● Usually reasonable working hours
● Very high staffing ratio (about 1:4)	● Staff ratio about 1:8
● Staff (unpaid) drawn from all walks of life	● Staff (paid) often outdoor or group work full-time trainers

Figure A1   Differences between VSL and traditional Outward Bound

VSL course using dramaturgy	Traditional Outward Bound course
• Multiple media — art, outdoors, music, video, drama, 'happenings', reflection and review	• Dominated by outdoor media, others also used. Planned and structured review after activity
• Constant on-course staff reflection, redesign of programme, evolving perception of delegates' needs	• Constant on-course staff reflection on whether the course is meeting its pre-agreed objectives
• Multiple (changing) objectives with an overall wide objective	• Objectives clearly fixed beforehand
• Programme subject to constant change to serve participants' needs	• Programme subject to some change if change is seen to meet objectives
• Surprises and unpredictable outcomes expected	• Predictable outcomes valued
• Participants do not know the programme beforehand	• Participants know programme beforehand
• Many of the activities framed in fantasy	• Mainly 'real' activities

Figure A2   Comparisons of dramaturgy and Outward Bound approaches

Source: Adapted from Krouwel, 2000, p.67

is developed by the chief instructor and their team, and new games are encouraged and trialled. This course individuality is known as an 'authored course'. Junior instructors, *elévs*, are included on the team as part of their training.

On traditional Outward Bound courses, participants depend physically on each other, and are usually involved in the chores and logistics of their group. A problem in the group dynamics can cause major difficulties during an expedition, so it is in the group's best interest to address them. Participants learn about each other through observing during activities, which include reviews. At VSL, the game element presents other forms of mutual interaction rather than just physical dependence, and in order to bring maximum impact for the participants they are often removed from the daily duties of the centre (maintenance, cooking, and so on). Most of the challenges are introduced through a simulated problem situation, but with real processes and impacts on the participants. Participants learn a lot about each other during activities, encompassing physical, psychological and emotional aspects, and are able to share on a deep emotional level relatively early on the course.

The traditional role of the Outward Bound instructor has been in the background, only stepping in when needed as a facilitator. Their role begins on the first day and finishes on the last. At VSL, the instructor is a part of the participant group. The line between instructor and participant is often blurred at times, although the instructor's role, responsibilities and ethical concerns remain in full effect, no matter how much they are involved in the activities as a participant. Instructors attempt to engage participants before the course starts by sending them specific tasks (framed as pre-course games), and after the course reunion activities are often initiated.

Bibliography

Anderson-Hanley, C. (1997). Adventure programming and spirituality: Integration models, methods, and research. *Journal of Experiential Education*, 20(2), 102–108.

Andresen, L., Boud, D., and Cohen, R. (1995). Experience based learning. In G. Foley (ed.), *Understanding Adult Education and Training* (pp.207–219). Sydney: Allen & Unwin.

Bacon, S. (1983). *The Conscious Use of Metaphor*. Denver: Colorado Outward Bound.

Bacon, S. (1987). *The Evolution of the Outward Bound Process*. Greenwich, CT: Outward Bound USA.

Beard, C., and Wilson, J.P. (2002). *The Power of Experiential Learning*. London: Kogan Page.

Belbin, R.M. (1981). *Management Teams: Why they Succeed or Fail*. Oxford: Butterworth Heinemann.

Boniface, M.R. (2000). Towards an understanding of flow and other positive experience phenomena within outdoor and adventurous activities. *Journal of Adventure Education and Outdoor Learning*, 1, 55–68.

Boud, D., Cohen, R., and Walker, D. (eds). (1993). *Using Experience for Learning*. Buckingham: Open University.

Bricháček, V. (1994). Prostřednictím výchovy. In Outward Bound Czech Republic: Prázdninová Škola Lipnice, *Instruktorský slabikář* (pp.11–24). Prague: Nadace Rozvoje Občanské Společnosti.

Broderick, A., and Pearce, G. (2001). Indoor adventure training: A dramaturgical approach to management development. *Journal of Organizational Change Management*, 14(3), 239–252.

Comenius, J.E. (1907). *The Great Didactic of John Amos Comenius, translated into English and edited with biographical, historical and critical introductions by M.W. Keatinge* (2nd ed.). London: Black (original work published 1632).

Comenius, J.E. (1998). *The Labyrinth of the World and the Paradise of the Heart*. New York: Paulist Press.

Csikszentmihalyi, M. (1991). *Flow: The psychology of optimal experience*. New York: Harper Perennial (originally published 1623).

Dewey, J. (1938/1965). *Experience and Education*. New York: Collier Books.

Dewey, J. (1916/1966). *Democracy and Education*. New York: Macmillan.

Dickson, T.J., Chapman, J., and Hurrell, M. (2000). Risk in the outdoors: The perception, the appeal, the reality. *Australian Journal of Outdoor Education*, 4(2), 10–17.

Doughty, S. (1991). Three generations of development training. *Journal of Adventure Education and Outdoor Leadership*, 7(4), 7–9.

Flor, R. (1991). Building bridges between organization development and experiential/adventure education. *Journal of Experiential Education*, 14(3), 27–34.

Gardner, H. (1983). *The Theory of Multiple Intelligences*. New York: Basic Books.

Gass, M.A. (1993). Foundations of adventure therapy. In M.A. Gass, *Adventure Therapy: Therapeutic application of adventure programming* (pp.3–10). Iowa: Kendall Hunt.

Gilsdorf, R. (1995). A workshop sequence in adventure education for German educators. *Journal of Experiential Education*, 18(3), 145–149.

Goleman, D. (1996). *Emotional Intelligence*. London: Bloomsbury.

Gray, J. (1992). *Men are from Mars, Women are from Venus*. New York: HarperCollins.

Greenaway, R. (1993). *Playback: A guide to reviewing activities*. Edinburgh: Callender Printers.

Handy, C. (1989). *The Age of Unreason*. London: Business Books.

Holec, O. (1994a). Dramaturgie. In Outward Bound Czech Republic: Prázdninová Škola Lipnice, *Instruktorský slabikář* (pp.37–50). Prague: Nadace Rozvoje Občanské Společnosti.

Holec, O. (1994b). The present and the future of Outward Bound Czech Republic. In J. Neumann, I. Mytting and J. Brtník (eds), *Outdoor Activities: Proceedings of international seminar Prague '94 Charles University* (pp.145–148). Lüneburg: Verlag Edition Erlebnispädagogik.

Hopkins, D., and Putnam, R. (1993). *Personal Growth Through Adventure*. London: David Fulton Publishers.

Hrkal, J., and Hanuš, R. (eds) (1998). *Zlatý fond her II*. Prague: Portál.

Hunt, J.S. (1990). The philosophy of adventure education. In J.C. Miles and S. Priest, *Adventure Education* (pp.119–128). State College, PA: Venture.

Itin, C.M. (1999). Reasserting the philosophy of experiential education as a vehicle for change in the 21st century. *Journal of Experiential Education*, 22(2), 91–98.

James, T. (1985). Sketch of a moving spirit: Kurt Hahn. In R. Kraft and M. Sakofs (eds), *The Theory of Experiential Education* (2nd ed.) (pp.39–44). Colorado: Association for Experiential Education.

James, T. (2000). Can the mountains speak for themselves? *Scisco Conscientia*, 3, 1–4 (original work published 1916).

Joplin, L. (1981). On defining experiential education. *Journal of Experiential Education*, 4(1), 17–20.

Knotek, M. (ed.) (2001). *Sborník instruktorského kursu* (Instructor course compendium). Praha: Prázdninová Škola Lipnice.

Kolb, D.A. (1984). *Experiential Learning: Experience as the source of learning and development*. Englewood Cliffs, NJ: Prentice Hall.

Kraft, R., and Sakofs, M. (eds) (1991). *The Theory of Experiential Education*. Boulder, CO: Association for Experiential Education.

Krouwel, W. (1994). The Czech way to personal development. *Training Officer*, 30(5), 140–142.

Krouwel, W. (2000). *An investigation into the past, current and potential role of outdoor development (and particularly outdoor management development) practice in Britain in the light of practice at Vacation School Lipnice and Česka cestá in the Czech Republic*. Unpublished master's thesis, University of Lancaster, UK.

Leberman, S.I., and Martin, A.J. (2002). Does pushing comfort zones produce the most learning? *Australian Journal of Outdoor Education*, 7(1), 71–81.

Leberman, S.I., and Martin, A.J. (2004a). Applying dramaturgy to management education. *Journal of Management Education* (in review).

Leberman, S.I., and Martin, A.J. (2004b). Enhancing transfer of learning through post course reflection. *Journal of Adventure Education and Outdoor Learning* (in review).

Luckmann, C. (1996). Defining experiential education. *Journal of Experiential Education*, 19(1), 6–7.

Luckner, J.L., and Nadler, R.S. (1997). *Processing the Experience: Strategies to enhance and generalize learning*. Dubuque, IO: Kendall Hunt.

Martin, A.J. (2000, July). Towards a new generation of Outward Bound. *Horizons: Journal of The Association for Outdoor Learning*, 10, 29–30.

Martin, A.J. (2001a). Outdoor adventure the Czech way. In M. Green (ed.), *12th National Outdoor Education Conference: Conference proceedings, January 15–18, LaTrobe University, Bendigo* (pp.101–108). Victoria, Australia: Victorian Outdoor Education Association.

Martin, A.J. (2001b). 'Dramaturgy': A holistic approach to outdoor education. *Australian Journal of Outdoor Education*, 5(2), 34–41.

Martin, A.J. (2001c). The dramaturgy wave. *Horizons*, 15, Autumn, 26–29.

Martin, A.J. (2001d). *Towards the Next Generation of Experiential Education Programmes: A case study of Outward Bound*. Unpublished doctoral thesis, Massey University, Palmerston North, New Zealand.

Martin, A.J. (2002). Creativity, innovation and a holistic program design. *Outward Bound International*, 10(1), 1,4.

Martin, A.J. (2003). Adding value to the Outward Bound educational process. *Outward Bound International*, 11(1), 4,5.

Martin, A.J., and Leberman, S.I. (2000). Adventure the Czech way [On-line]. *Scisco Conscientia*, 2(3), 1–17.

Martin, A.J., Leberman, S.I., and Neill, J.T. (2002). Dramaturgy as a method for experiential program design. *Journal of Experiential Education*, 25(1), 196–206.

Maslow, A.H. (1962). *Toward a Psychology of Being*. Princeton, NJ: Van Nostrand.

Mossman, A. (1983). Making choices about the use of outdoors in management development. *Management Education and Development*. 14(3), 182–196.

Nadler, R.S. (1995). Edgework: Stretching boundaries and generalizing experiences. *Journal of Experiential Education*, 18(1), 52–55.

Neuman, J. (2001a). The Czech way of outdoor experiential education. In F.H. Paffrath and A. Ferstl (eds), *Hemingsles erleben* (pp.329–338). Augsberg: Ziel.

Neuman, J. (2001b). Introduction to outdoor education in the Czech Republic. In A-C. Nilsson (ed.), *Outdoor Education: Authentic learning in the context of landscapes* (pp.31–41). Kisa, Sweden: Kinda Education.

Petrová, O., Horáková, S., Mikšíčková, J. and Bláha, J. (1999). *Czech Report*. Canberra: Outward Bound Australia and Outward Bound Czech Republic.

Prázdninová Škola Lipnice (1990). *Zlatý fond her*. Prague: Mladá Fronta.

Prázdninová Škola Lipnice (1994). *Instruktorský slabikář*. Prague: Nadace Rozvoje Občanské Společnosti.

Priest, S. (1990). The adventure experience paradigm. In J.C. Miles and S. Priest (eds), *Adventure Education* (pp.157–162). State College, PA: Venture.

Priest, S., and Gass, M.A. (1993). Five generations of facilitated learning from adventure experiences. *Journal of Adventure Education and Leadership*, 10(3), 23–25.

Priest, S., and Gass, M.A. (1997). *Effective Leadership in Adventure Programming*. Champaign, IL: Human Kinetics.

Reynolds, M. (1998). *Reflection and Critical Reflection in Management Learning*. Thousand Oaks, CA: Sage.

Richards, A. (1990). Kurt Hahn. In J.C. Miles and S. Priest (eds), *Adventure Education* (pp. 67–74). State College, PA: Venture.

Richards, A. (1994). From exposure to engagement or awareness to action. *Journal of Adventure Education and Outdoor Leadership*, 11(2), 6–8.

Rohnke, K. (1984). *Silver Bullets*. Hamilton, MA: Project Adventure.

Sadler, J.E. (ed.) (1969). *Comenius*. London: Collier-Macmillan.

Sakofs, M., and Armstrong, G.P. (1996). *Into the Classroom: The Outward Bound approach to teaching and learning*. Dubuque, IA: Kendall/Hunt.

Schoel, J., Prouty, D., and Radcliffe, P. (1988). *Islands of Healing: A guide to adventure based counselling*. Hamilton, MA: Project Adventure.

Shantz, C. (1998). *Dictionary of the Theatre: Terms, concepts and analysis*. Toronto: University of Toronto.

Stetson, C.P. (1996). *Journey with Kurt Hahn*. Victoria, Canada: Outward Bound International.

Strugatsky, A., and Strugatsky, B. (1979). *Roadside Picnic*. London: Penguin.

Turčová, I., Neuman, J., and Martin, A.J. (2003). The outdoors from a Czech perspective. *Horizons*, 24, 26–29.

Valenta, J. (1995). *Kapitoly z teorie výchovné dramatiky*. Praha: ISV.

Waic, M., and Kössl, J. (1994). The origin and development of organized outdoor activities in the Czech countries. In J. Neuman, I. Mytting and J. Brtník (eds), *Outdoor Activities: Proceedings of international seminar Prague '94 Charles University* (pp.18–22). Lüneburg: Verlag Edition Erlebnispädagogik.

Walsh, V., and Golins, G. (1976). *The Exploration of the Outward Bound Process Model*. Denver: Colorado Outward Bound.

Wurdinger, S. (1994). Examining the learning process used in adventure education. *Journal of Adventure Education and Outdoor Leadership*, 11(3), 25–27.

Wyndham, J. (1986). *The Day of the Triffids*. New York: Ballantine Books (originally published 1951).

Zink, R., and Leberman, S.I. (2001). Risking a debate – Redefining risk and risk management: A New Zealand case study. *Journal of Experiential Education*, 24(1), 50–57.

Index